W9-CRT-221

DEDICATION

To my father John and my sister Lygia. Both of you taught me by example; that making a sale is always about helping people solve real problems.

This single idea has shaped my life.

TABLE OF CONTENTS

*The Market
Has Changed
Have You?*

Paul D'Souza

FOREWORD

When we set out to sell something in the marketplace, most of us focus on the transaction, on the deal. We want to make it stick and make our money. Obviously, these fundamentals make sales and business happen, and these goals are, for obvious reasons, quite appropriate. Yet, there is more that can be done to increase the quality of the transaction and our profit margins. Paul talks about all this—offering you a better chance to succeed in tough and changing markets, and showing you how to achieve higher levels of long-term profitability.

In my experiences at Joie de Vivre (the second largest boutique hotelier in the country), we do just that—the PEAK business model suggests that we address customer expectations at the first level of interaction, but that we then move to communicate with and understand our customers so that we begin to fulfill their unrecognized or unexpressed needs that the customers themselves might not have known could be met by us. We seek to give them "peak experiences"; in essence, all of us—from our sales team to the entire organization—strive to be mind readers of what our customers actually want and expect. Our ability to listen, and our attention to detail and awareness of what we are doing, move our customer relationships way beyond a transaction and into the realm of a long-term partnership, engendering tremendous loyalty. Customers come back over and over again to have these peak experiences. Paul's **Wha-Dho** philosophy and approach to life and business is nested in these very same ideas. His fifth principle, Practical Leadership, speaks to this idea particularly, and you will find it very empowering.

We need more people thinking like this. Everything has changed in the marketplace, and it's time for us to respond. We need to take this conversation of business and how we approach our customers to a new level of interaction—one is anchored in clear thinking and recognizing that as people we are all in it together. Paul brings the conversation of sales and business back to the individual, and he suggests that we take the initiative to be clear about who we are as people and what we want to accomplish. This approach gives us the ability to act with power everywhere and in everything we do.

As individuals, of course, we cannot accomplish much if we do not build loyalty and long-term relationships with our friends, employers, customers, and partners. At Joie de Vivre, we have always moved beyond the transactional nature of interaction, because transactional profits—if that's all there are—can be very costly in the long run. Building loyalty at every level is the surest way to increase and maintain your revenue and your profits.

I like how Paul includes a Practice Exercise toward the end of every principle. These give you immediate and practical insight on how you can incorporate the ideas from the book into your life.

I believe this book will transform you when you apply its ideas. Read it, and arm yourself with the skills, attitudes, and insights that will help you succeed in not just a tough market, but in any market.

This is the real deal, folks. Paul's book offers new thinking and practices that will help you navigate through the tough markets we find ourselves in today. Yet, on a broader level, markets will always be changing. We cannot survive just by taking orders and riding the wave of market growth. In these markets, we have to identify needs, work with our partners and customers, and solve real problems that give our customers an exceptional value in the offers we make them. We have to give them peak experiences that make them want to come back for more. After all, is that not why we are in business?

I admire Paul's commitment to working with the fundamental idea that it is people that make things happen in business. I also love his suggesting that to do more in the realm of sales and revenue generation, one has to be a better person, a better businessperson, and a consummate professional. We have grown our business at Joie de Vivre by embracing this idea. Our employees, our customers, and our investors need to be fulfilled and self-expressed at every step. It is gratifying to see Paul bring attention to this way of thinking to the word of sales and salesmanship. He truly has identified the heartbeat of all business.

Chip Conley
Author; Founder and CEO
Joie de Vivre Hospitality
www.chipconley.com

BOOK ENDORSEMENTS

"Our compliments to Paul D'Souza for a valuable contribution to the new movement toward professionalizing sales.

"D'Souza has recognized that true professionals—physicians, engineers, attorneys, and especially salespeople—share three critical characteristics:

The Market Has Changed Have You?

Paul D'Souza

1. They recognize that a profession is first and foremost a career, a journey, and a commitment to a mission
2. The journey is about the quality of the trip, its purpose and standards, not the destination; and perhaps most critically
3. The commitment is personal: to satisfy yourself more than impressing others; to enjoy the respect of those you have served; and to achieve the pride of having contributed more to this world than you have taken out.

"His advice is sound, and not surprisingly is equally appropriate for all professionals...not just sales!"

Howard Stevens
CEO of HR Chally
President of the University Sales Education Foundation (USEF)

"A tough economy brings out tough behaviors in customers. This recession has been tougher on salespeople since it runs parallel to a dramatic shift in the world of selling. Information technology and social networking have changed the buying process. Salespeople need to adapt their selling styles to the new way of buying. This book offers concrete steps that can help salespeople adapt their approach to the way customers buy while dealing with the tougher customer whose behavior has been hardened by the recession economy. A must read for sales professionals committed to winning."

Gerhard Gschwandtner
Founder and Publisher
Selling Power (www.sellingpower.com)

"Every organization will benefit when their employees grow, personally and professionally. Paul's book addresses just that. The part I liked most is that while the book provides a framework for salespeople to be effective in their jobs, it also (simultaneously) presents an opportunity for them to grow personally in their lives. It's a double-win."

Rajesh Setty
Entrepreneur, Author, and Speaker
www.rajeshsetty.com

"Paul D'Souza's approach to sales is both practical and insightful. He presents a rare mixture of solid and actionable sales advice with deeper wisdom into what challenges and motivates all of us when we are involved in the sales process."

Hanley Brite
Principal and Founder, Authentic Connections, Inc.
www.authenticconnections.com

"This is truly the practical success guide of our generation. If an individual can change how they think and interact with others, they can change their ability to sell and profit from those sales. Paul has created the perfect tool to direct all businesspeople to a new way of succeeding in the marketplace."

Jim Switzenberg, CEC
Culinary Arts Instructor and Restaurant Consultant
www.chefswitz.com

"Business leaders need pragmatic advice that can be applied in growing their business, not lofty management theories and ideas that only apply to the largest multinationals. Paul's book is practical, holistic, and will offer you ideas that will help your bottom line."

Mark Faust
Founder, Echelon Management
www.echelonmanagement.com

"Paul does an exceptional job at not only helping salespeople understand what to do in economic challenged times but also makes them THINK about what to do. It's one thing to read a book and act on the instructions in the book on how to improve. It's an entirely different instance to THINK about what to change and UNDERSTAND why you need to change. That's really how to imbed change long term. Paul does that for us here."

Daniel Perry
VP Sales
Lavi Industries
www.lavi.com

"Paul's approach is designed to help you focus on the things you can do yourself to achieve better sales performance in a changing business environment. But more than that, he helps you build a strong foundation for that time when things change again. And we know they will."

Denis Clark
Senior Executive, Entrepreneur, Business Advisor
www.denisclark.com

"This is a good read! Paul has captured the essence of great salesmanship: understanding yourself, your client, and your environment. The balance he offers is appropriate for tough markets, and even more essential when times are good— when your customers need relationships they can trust. This book should be required reading for all consultants and sales professionals."

Benjamin Harris III
Senior Account Executive
Fortune 100 Company

"Paul D'Souza's 25 Steps will save you from spinning your wheels in sales and help you achieve the traction to power out of this recession through effective self-management and sales. Paul helps readers 'slow down to speed up' and tap into their individual creative genius and drive us forward to a better future."

David Parks
Vice President, Business Development
Blue Point Leadership
www.bluepointleadership.com

"When the going gets tough, the tough get going. But how? When? Why? And which precious few actions and habits can help you thrive through tough times to build your business? Paul D'Souza answers all these questions and many more in this indispensable book. Read it, apply it, and never languish again."

Lisa Haneberg
Vice President, MPI Consulting;
Author of 10 business books
www.lisahaneberg.com

"I really like Paul's stand...'When you are clear about what you want to accomplish, you will bring more passion and creativity.' This applies in every instance of successful selling, and even more so when selling in tough markets. This is a must read for everyone in sales."

Peter Purushotma
Founding Director
Singapore American Business Association.

"Having worked directly with Paul, I can tell you that he has a keen insight into the sales process. Just as Paul did with my sales efforts, Paul can help turn your career in the right direction. I believe the **Wha-Dho** sales strategy laid out in this book, can help you and your team meet you business and life goals."

Jared Willis
Director of Sales
BarkerBlue Digital

"This is a transformation book and a guide for high-performers. Paul has taken the guesswork out of achieving extraordinary results. Put this book on your must-read list if you want to learn how to take performance to a higher level no matter what the market conditions. Paul has helped pave the path to the next level of professionalism, a book filled with useful advise, insights and tactics that will propel you to success."

Irina Haydon
Executive Director of Sales
Heartland Payment Systems

INTRODUCTION

The market has changed—have you? Over the past few years, our markets have experienced rapid transformation: changes driven by financial conditions, macroeconomics, geopolitical change, and technological innovation. Yet our need to make a sale and generate profit remains the same. Life goes on.

The Market Has Changed Have You?

Paul D'Souza

You must still put food on the table, feel passionate about your work, and fulfill your responsibility to produce revenue for your business. Are you asking yourself any of these questions:

- What do I do now?
- How do we fill the pipeline?
- How do we increase our close ratios?
- What is our strategy moving forward?

If you answered yes to any of these questions, then this book is for you. It was written for anyone who has a revenue commitment in some shape or form. You know who you are!

I put you at heart of the sales life cycle—you, the salesperson that serves as the foundation of all sales activity. In this book, I give you a strategy that works and 25 steps you can use to increase your productivity in this tough marketplace.

Most selling systems seem to think that salespeople live only to sell. These programs treat salespeople as pushbutton automatons who should make 100 cold calls every day to keep their sales pipeline full. While this by-the-numbers formula does work and produces sales, it completely ignores the critical fact that salespeople are, first and foremost, people.

I wrote this book for...

- Sales professionals with less than 10 years' experience.
- Sales leaders—you can use this book as a training tool.
- Real estate and insurance agents.
- Small-business owners.
- Forced entrepreneurs.
- Physicians, dentists, chiropractors, and therapists.
- Restaurateurs, event planners, and caterers.
- Retailers of every kind.
- Investment bankers and relationship managers.
- Multilevel marketing professionals.

In a changing marketplace, you need two elements: you need a strategy that awakens the power that resides within you (in your heart) and you also need the science of sales.

In this book, you will find strategic guidelines and practical exercises you can leverage right away to help you close deals and make money. At the end of the day, I want you to have a better life as well as a better revenue number.

WHAT IS THE **WHA-DHO** PHILOSOPHY?

The **Wha-Dho** philosophy is a body of knowledge and a way of thinking that I created after studying human awareness, economic principles, and business practices for the last 20 years. **Wha-Dho** means "The Way of Harmony" in Japanese, which allows organizations and people to achieve higher levels of success and prosperity by harmonizing these three business domains:

*The Market
Has Changed
Have You?*

Paul D'Souza

1. The people involved in your business (human capital).
2. Economic principles that apply.
3. Business practices that relate to your market.

Where these three ideas meet and work together, you will find revenue, profitability, and sustainable success. In other words, you will find "harmony."

At its core, the **Wha-Dho** sales philosophy focuses on leverage. It will help you leverage everything—the full array of assets and relationships you have access to. When you follow **Wha-Dho**, you will succeed in booming marketplaces, stable marketplaces, and even changing marketplaces.

Today's marketplaces experience unceasing evolutionary pressures. Customer behavior constantly changes; government regulations change; and your competitors innovate. As a salesperson, you must be prepared to thrive in such an environment. You cannot expect to succeed merely through good luck and hard work. You need a deeper guiding strategy that is anchored in purpose behind your actions.

Having used **Wha-Dho** to help quite a few companies and thousands of people increase revenue, I have seen people achieve these fundamental results:

1. They improve revenue and profit margins;
2. They improve their careers; and
3. They improve themselves as people.

You might initially think that the first and second outcomes will naturally lead to the third result. Yet, I will argue that the change must come the other way around. When you improve yourself as a person, you have greater impact as a salesperson, and as a result, your sales and profits will improve.

Wha-Dho, at its core, creates a conversation of power—one in which you can solve real problems and act more powerfully. You will learn how to align your every thought, word, and action with your core values and current objectives.

Everyday you make choices in your personal life and at work. The choices you make, will either support what you do or they will sabotage your efforts. The Wha-Dho sales strategy shows you how to make choices that will align your sales activity with you personal and business objectives. This is power in action, this creates harmony.

18

At every juncture possible, I will show you how to be effective, efficient, and powerful—both as a person and a salesperson. As a result, you will be able to achieve your goals and live your dreams. You owe yourself that.

*The Market
Has Changed
Have You?*

Paul D'Souza

You have probably picked up this book because you are looking for answers to help you close more deals today. You want to be more effective in a changing and tough sales environment. Immediate action is required.

The Market Has Changed Have You?

Paul D'Souza

This book will help you make the changes you need to be productive and profitable now and into the future.

You can read this book from cover to cover in one or two sittings, or you can invest small daily windows of time to work on specific chapters. I would advise you to do both. Take the time to work through this book. It will change your life.

The book is organized in five parts, each discussing one of the Five Principles of the **Wha-Dho** sales strategy. They are:

1. The Principle of **Purpose**

2. The Principle of **Prosperity**

3. The Principle of **Process**

4. The Principle of **People**

5. The Principle of **Practical Leadership**

Each of these parts contains five steps that you can use to increase your ability to close deals. I have also included a Practice Exercise for every one of the 25 Steps. You will be able to use these exercises to strengthen your skills and be effective in the real-world within minutes.

Apply these ideas in your life and see how the principles of **Wha-Dho** can move you to places of power and prosperity. Join the thousands of others who have enjoyed this guide, and use it to achieve the success you deserve.

The Market Has Changed Have You?

Paul D'Souza

Part 1

THE PRINCIPLE OF PURPOSE

Step 1: WHAT DO YOU WANT TO ACCOMPLISH?

Step 2: MAKE A COMMITMENT TO WIN

Step 3: MANAGE YOUR MOOD

Step 4: REACH BEYOND YOURSELF

Step 5: LEVERAGE YOUR SUPPORT TEAMS

What are you committed to accomplishing in life, this year, this quarter, or this month? Your actions today must align with your long-term goals for you to achieve them.

This first part focuses on your vision and sense of purpose in life. You need a strategy for yourself. Awaken the dragon within, tap into your creative genius, and control your destiny. You need to be clear about what you are committed to accomplishing. When that is done, you can begin to move toward that goal—powerfully, effectively, and profitably.

The Market Has Changed Have You?

The Principle of Purpose

Many other sales books focus on the process instead of the person. This book places you—and your goals—at the core of the entire **Wha-Dho** philosophy of sales.

If you want to be effective in the marketplace, then you must be clear about what your passion and commitments are. Only then will you accomplish your goals, fulfill your dreams, and live the life you have always wanted to live.

Do any items in this list resemble your personal goals?

- I have a specific number for retirement.
- I need to put my children through college.
- I want to spend more time with my family.
- I want to do more charity and volunteer work.
- I want to raise funds and start a new business.

Why do anything that does not support your vision and the commitments you have made to yourself and your family?

Our exploration of **Wha-Dho** begins with the Principle of Purpose, and we will focus on you as a person. Once this fundamental idea has taken root in your mind and your heart, you will move rapidly toward your goals and your vision. You will be able to assess, quickly and with confidence, whether your actions will support your goals or work to actually sabotage them.

In this part, I want you to explore your purpose for doing anything at all. **Wha-Dho** requires that you commit yourself to purposeful actions. You may not find any magical shortcuts, but you will find access to powerful internal forces that make you more effective, day in and day out.

When you are clear about what you want to accomplish, you will bring more passion and creativity to your work. Instead of feeling weary and worn, your heart will be engaged and full of energy. You will be driven and filled with passion and enthusiasm, simply because you will know where you are going at all times.

Step 1

WHAT DO YOU WANT TO ACCOMPLISH?

If you want to achieve success in your life or your career, then you need to be absolutely clear about your goals.

The Market Has Changed Have You?

The Principle of Purpose

As a salesperson, you probably have specific sales goals and revenue targets. During the good times, these goals seemed achievable and realistic. However, you have now found yourself in a changing sales environment. It may become harder to find leads, and you may have to work harder to close deals. The sales cycle has stretched itself out, and your sales pipeline may feel lean compared to past years. Your initial goals may seem out of reach or even unrealistic. When the going gets tough, do not take it personally; challenging sales environments can occur for many reasons:

- A change in economic conditions;
- A change in your specific market segment;
- A change in government regulations;
- A change in consumer preference; or
- A change in the competitive landscape because of a fundamental shift in the marketplace.

These are just a few reasons that will make a sales environment feel tougher than it used to be. When faced with this situation, you might be tempted to blame external forces. After all, it's easy to blame other factors, such as the economy or competitors.

Many salespeople ask the wrong question, wondering "Why did this happen to me?"

Instead of assigning blame to others, empower yourself by saying, "My sales world has changed. How should I change to adapt to this new environment? What can I accomplish with these new market conditions?"

I want to ask you two elemental questions:

- What are you trying to accomplish in the marketplace as a generator of revenue?
- What motivates you? Fear, passion, or a deep sense of wanting to accomplish something of significance?

If you are driven by fear, then you will act reactively instead of proactively. Fear provides a weak mental position for any salesperson. When a sales environment changes or becomes difficult, I encourage salespeople to return to the basics and look within themselves to overcome their fear.

Let's say that you are responsible for producing a given revenue target. What I suggest, is you start by finding personal meaning in what you are committed to doing. This alone will help you tap into your creativity, passion and resourcefulness.

Of course, it is always good to be clear about your career goals as well as the salary, commissions, and bonuses that you might want to earn. But what I am really referring to here is a more personal story, indicated by the following questions:

- What is it you want to accomplish in life?
- What is it that motivates you?
- What are you passionate about?

Sometimes, you will focus on the necessities, such as money for medical insurance for yourself or your children. Or, you might look forward to a $400 monthly bonus check that allows you to pursue one of your hobbies.

Your motivation might also be totally unrelated to finances in any way. You might just love doing what you do and enjoy selling your product or service. The important thing to know, though, is that when you identify motivators that matter to you, they will energize you, fuel your enthusiasm, and sustain you through both good times and bad.

Practice Exercise

Invest time in the practice of "Active Inactivity." Do this regularly; it will help you stay grounded in what is important to you.

Here's what to do:

Devote a half-day or full day away from work, family, and friends. Turn off your phone and ignore your e-mails. Spend that time alone doing absolutely nothing. Do not try to run errands or fill your time with chores. Instead, use this time to look inside yourself and ask yourself tough questions. Do not accept glib or easy answers. Dig deep; look within; and find what truly matters to you.

Perhaps you want to provide for your family. What does "provide" look like? Quantify it. If you say you want the financial resources to live a good life, assign numbers (either monthly income or net worth) to define your goals.

- I sell because…
- I want to accomplish…
- I am motivated by…
- I am passionate about…

The clearer your motivations, the more powerfully you will be able to conduct yourself in the marketplace. Do not let yourself write vague answers, because only strong motivation, driven by specific goals, will provide you the energy you need to thrive in a changing market.

One final note. Knowing what you want to accomplish sets the space for you to act. From this point forward you will have direction and a sense of purpose.

Step 2

In a changing sales marketplace, no salesperson wins by just show-ing up, and no customer waits for salespeople to appear. Most successful sales contracts require a lot of work in good economic times. Imagine how attentive you have to be when you're selling in a tough market.

Your commitment to win will distinguish you from your competi-tors in the marketplace. You absolutely need to be energized, en-thusiastic, attentive, and confident—believing that you will over-come any obstacle that might come your way.

You must dig deep into your psyche and pull out a winning solu-tion that brings that deal home. You have got to put your heart into it. Because if you don't, you will be just like all your other competi-tors—another salesperson making noise.

When people lack a deep sense of commitment, they can become frustrated and despair easily about the change process. They might even fail to recognize the need to change and the opportunities that lie before them—until it's too late.

However, with the right attitude, you might discover fantastic op-portunities lying before you. You will be able to design more pow-erful solutions that leverage the experiences and the resources you already have. Markets will change and evolve constantly, and these changes might not always align with your business forecasts or

The Market Has Changed Have You?

The Principle of Purpose

schedules; you may, in fact, find yourself completely unprepared for how the market moves. Yet you have to succeed. You have to win.

Case in Point

The Market Has Changed Have You?

Paul D'Souza

SourceSelect, a third-party logistics company in Silicon Valley, took advantage of the 2008 recession to reshape its offerings to customers, who viewed carrying warehouse space, assembly lines, and shipping expenses as exceptionally burdensome overhead during the recession. Mahaveer Jain, the CEO, crafted a new marketing campaign that positioned the company's offering as an on-demand solution for its customers, allowing them to purchase production lines, warehouse space, and fulfillment services whenever they needed. This offering allowed SourceSelect's customers to lower their overhead costs, decrease financial risks, and reduce late-night headaches at a time when they were struggling with decreased demand. SourceSelect created a very powerful offer that helped its customers manage their risks when the marketplace collapsed. Result? Even though the market was in freefall, SourceSelect grew revenue 30% that quarter.

Mahaveer's commitment to win gave the company a competitive edge. They acted creatively. They restructured and redesigned their strategies when they recognized things had changed.

When you have a commitment to win, you will find ways to sustain and grow your revenues. Cash flow is like oxygen. In business, very little matters or survives without it. In some ways, you might equate your commitment to win with your "will to live."

Whether you serve as the company's CEO or its most junior salesperson, this sense of commitment is essential in business. When

30

the market changes, so must you—your strategy, your tactics and what you sell. The buck starts and stops with you.

The recent global recession created an incredibly challenging sales environment. Few salespeople have ever seen markets this tight. Very few people had the experiences and skills they needed to achieve success.

For years, we had been taking orders and riding the coattails of our partners and vendors. The market had momentum because people had access to financial resources. Then, the situation changed suddenly. People became reluctant to ink a deal.

Mark Montanaro of Chateaux Software notes that contracts often require at least seven revisions before they will be signed by customers. He also notes that this practice has become more the rule than the exception.

Do you have what it takes to do good business in today's markets? You and your partners must possess a serious commitment to win.

The market has changed—have you? How will these changes reshape your business? How are you going to change personally? What has got to give—for you to get to be successful? You and everybody else you work with closely have got to rise to the occasion and make a commitment to win. You must dig deeper than you have in the recent past. Go to a deeper place of power and resourcefulness. Make a personal commitment to yourself and each other to engage with a new sense of purpose and a commitment to win. It's time to do things right!

Practice Exercise

Your commitment to win must come from your core personal goals. If you simply choose a business agenda, then you will lack passion and energy. You need a strong motivator.

Envision a future that you would like to make happen. Link that event directly to something you want to accomplish in the marketplace now. You will activate your commitment to win. Here are some examples:

Could It Be Personal?
Example: You want to open a coffee shop in April 2013. For that to happen, you need to make $150,000 every year in 2010, 2011, and 2012.

Could It Be Family?
Example: You want to move your family to a better community by 2020.

Could It Be Philanthropic?
Example: You want to support a certain charitable organization in a significant way.

Your Answer:
I am committed to win, because I want to...

_____

_____

_____

Step 3

MANAGE YOUR MOOD

You have made a commitment to win. To do this, however, you also need to eliminate negative moods and focus on positive moods. Negative moods can sabotage all of your efforts in a changing market. As a salesperson, your moods are everything. Simply put, the longer you stay in a positive mood, the more effective you will be.

Your mood becomes especially important in changing sales environments. In tough times, you may hear negative news about your vertical space and the economy at large—declining sales numbers, increasing inventory, layoff announcements, and rising unemployment. When one or two people in your group slip into negative moods, they can very easily pull down others with them; keep your moods positive and morale high.

Your moods create the space of possibility for you to act or not. If you are in a good mood, one that abounds in energy and possibility, then people around you—like your customers and prospects—will be drawn to you. They will be influenced by your mood, and respond accordingly. Your powerful mood will also change the very nature of the thoughts you have and act on.

Negative moods cause more damage than you might expect. Your negative thoughts will begin to reinforce the fear and frustration you are feeling. You will become your own worst enemy, and success will not be yours.

The Market Has Changed Have You?

The Principle of Purpose

When marketplaces change, people tend to focus on the opportunities that are no longer possible. Fed by the media, many people at work talk about the drama in the marketplace; they are gripped by it and want you to be gripped by it as well. Be wary of this trap, and stay away from such discussions of despair.

Sure, times are tough, but life goes on. People still breathe, eat, sleep, work, feed their families, live in homes, and do whatever else they have to do. When the marketplace changes, the nature of business changes. Yet, business continues. Some sectors will most definitely decline, but wherever there are people, there will be markets.

There is work to do. There are deals to be made. You absolutely can control your mood and shape your future.

- Are you gripped by fear or negativity?
- How do you feel when you start your day?
- Are you aware of your moods throughout the day?

I encourage you to use persistence and willpower to make big changes in small shifts. Replace your negative moods—such as despair, fear, depression, anxiety, and worthlessness—with positive, productive moods—such as joy, happiness, excitement, and confidence.

Take stock of your mental and emotional strength as it relates to your business and career. Harness your emotions, strengthen your desire, and control your mood. You can do it if you:

- Choose your mood. Recognize your negative moods and release them.
- Quit people that bring you down.

34

- Uncomplicate your life—remove what's not real.
- Learn behavior from powerful people.
- Control your emotions and move to places of power.

Keep working this list until you can achieve a positive mood at will.

Practice Exercise

The Market Has Changed Have You?

In the business of sales, it is helpful to hold the following moods:

The Principle of Purpose

- Adventure
- Seductiveness
- Wonder
- Joy
- Creativity
- Gregarious enthusiasm

Question One
What adjectives would you use to describe your recent moods?

Question Two
What adjectives would other people currently use to describe you?

If you do not know, ask your friends and peers. Look for people who will be objective.

Now that you have had practice in noticing and changing your moods, choose powerful ones that will help you accomplish your goals:

- Be attentive, so you may notice opportunities.
- Be curious, so you may discover opportunities.

- Be focused, so you may move powerfully.
- Be kind, so you can transact easily.

Question Three
What moods do you want to hold moving forward?

When you achieve a positive mood, you will find that your attitude makes people want to be around you. Customers will begin to trust and open up to you, you will become a magnet for positive things, and you will succeed. Gregarious enthusiasm becomes infectious and useful in business to win and succeed. Harness that energy and watch the world bow to your desires.

Step 4

REACH BEYOND YOURSELF

If you want to move powerfully in a changing marketplace, you must be ready to reach beyond yourself and go that extra mile—or two. Anchor yourself in an idea and a dream that is bigger than who you are. In his book *Good to Great,* Jim Collins explores how companies and individuals set "Big Hairy Audacious Goals." These goals, which often defy conventional wisdom, typically seek to redefine the world (or at least your corner of it).

The Market Has Changed Have You?

The Principle of Purpose

Think about people who have changed the world in the last century. You might come up with individuals such as Steve Jobs of Apple, Sir Richard Branson of Virgin, and Herb Kelleher of Southwest Airlines, as well as the geniuses of Google, Larry Page and Sergey Brin. All of them reached beyond themselves and accomplished much. None of them started off successful.

Nothing of significance was ever created by being simple, conventional, or living in survival mode. Everything that is significant and valuable today came from thinking that was greater and far beyond what was normal and accepted at the time it was first proposed. Most of today's valuable ideas had their roots in ridiculous, unrealistic, grandiose, extravagant, and outright crazy thinking—crazy except to the person who stuck with it and made it happen.

People do extraordinary things when they reach beyond themselves. Think of Martin Luther King, Mahatma Gandhi, and Mother Teresa. These three people came from very humble origins, but they developed powerful voices because their vision extended beyond themselves. They held on to dreams much bigger than themselves, and they accomplished quite a lot in their lives.

Now, you might say, "But Paul, I'm a salesperson trying to sell something in a changing market. I'm not fighting for civil rights in the United States; I'm not seeking independence for India; and I'm not establishing hospice services for the poor and sick." You might even tell me that business has been so tough you do not have time to reach beyond yourself, because you just need to survive and get through this bad spell.

Yes, I agree. You are a salesperson, just trying to survive, and you may think that is all you can do. Let me show you how these two ideas—surviving a changing market and reaching beyond yourself—come together. Simply put, when you can reach beyond yourself, you will distinguish yourself from the mediocrity that surrounds you and you will begin to engage in thinking that surpasses your current activity level.

Case in Point

Allow me to go back into the nonprofit arena and show you how Mother Teresa was, without a doubt, one of the greatest salespeople of the 20th century. Here is the short version of her story.

She initially joined an existing religious order, the Sisters of Loretto. She felt a call to care for the sick and the poor. Many within her religious order thought her ideas were impractical and even outrageous. So, she left and formed her own order—the Sisters of Charity.

Mother Teresa stopped looking at things at the local level, and she began looking at things at a global level. She reached beyond herself and created the space for people to act—some people supported her financially, fellow nuns joined her in her work, and many others came in as volunteers. Millions of people bought into her vision of how the world could and should be. She showed people how to love and how to serve others.

If you think you have a challenging sales environment, imagine Mother Teresa's challenges. She sold her vision every day to every person she came in contact with, convincing people to spend their hard-earned money and scarce time to care for the sick and the dying. She was fantastic at asking for help. In fact, she was legendary at getting people to say yes to the demanding requests she made of them.

We had the opportunity of having Mother Teresa visit our home a few times, when she was building her center in Madras (now called Chennai), India. She asked my mother and father if they would host the monthly project planning meetings in our home. My mother still talks about how Mother Teresa would always push the envelope with her requests. She knew how to enroll people and get them to support her. Mother Teresa had a quiet but powerful way of asking people to do things for her and her cause. She framed her requests so powerfully that people invariably accepted and said yes.

Let the humanity of Mother Teresa stand out. Look at her story from the perspective of her ability to enroll people to take action to solve problems. I submit to you that all sales is just that, and exactly that—solving problems. To me, Mother Teresa was a highly effective salesperson who just happened to work in the non-profit sector.

Practice Exercise

What drives you to succeed? What empowers you to win? What fuels your resourcefulness? Are you holding an idea that is bigger than who you are?

Write the idea down and reconnect with it now. Reach beyond yourself. Make a stand!

_____

_____

_____

_____

_____

If you are not clear about what motivates you and drives you to succeed, I would suggest you work on identifying with something that has the power to move you.

Schedule some alone time. Sit comfortably, take a few deep breaths, and silence your mind. Bring your attention to your body and how you are feeling. Journey inward and reflect on the following questions:

- Do you love what you do?
- Have you been ignoring your "life calling"?
- Do you have a message you need to share with the world?

Step 5

LEVERAGE YOUR SUPPORT TEAMS

By now you should have developed a good idea of what you want to accomplish, and a clear sense of purpose. Before you put your plan into action, run it by your business partners. We all have people that influence what we do, and it's time to enlist them in your story. These people will include your business partners, who help you win deals, as well as your friends and family, who support you in life. Stay with the people you trust.

In addition, you need help from people who have lived through similar market conditions—people who have relevant experiences, people who can support you in reducing and managing risk, and people who can help you reach higher and do more.

How can you get these powerful people to help you? Under what conditions would they consider helping you out? These conditions generally fall in four criteria:

- Attraction—when you are attractive enough to get their attention.
- Value—when you have something valuable to offer them.
- Reciprocity—when you obligate them to help you back.
- Character—when it's from their own goodness.

Randy Pozos, author, health care consultant, and entrepreneur, once told me that "Humility is knowing your true worth." Once you learn to be truly humble, you will be able to notice and observe

The Market Has Changed Have You?

The Principle of Purpose

where you need help. With this awareness, you can go to your network of friends and associates and get the help you need to win in the marketplace.

Experience has taught me to initially focus closely on understanding the problems I face. Once I do, I can reach out to people and get the appropriate help I need to solve them. When I can connect with the right people, they will help me review and validate my plan of action, making sure it's the right one—before I start implementing change.

Case in Point

A few years ago, I worked with a digital printing company that produced large-format construction drawings, small-format prints, and short-run, print-on-demand jobs that competed with Kinko's. When I took over as vice president of sales, I had no idea how the print industry worked. In addition, I had no existing contacts in the industry, yet I had committed to growing revenue and increasing profits.

I started working with everyone in the company, from the management and sales team to the customer service and production teams, as well as the drivers who delivered the prints to the customers. I talked to all of them, learning and understanding what they did and asking them a key question:

What would you do to increase revenue here?

Everyone I asked provided a wealth of information. Armed with this first level of industry information, I reached out to our customers. First, I spoke with customers who were very happy with our services. Then, I talked with customers who had not used us

42

recently. I asked them a similar question: How could we work with you better?

And they told me! They told me what was important to them. In essence, they told me how to sell to them. Inside of 90 days, our revenues began to increase.

Learn to empower people around you to help you accomplish whatever it is you are committed to doing. Never forget that the people in your life are the force multipliers who can help you accomplish more.

Practice Exercise

Inventory the skills and the resources you have to offer people, as well as the resources of the people you know. How are you leveraging these connections?

*The Market
Has Changed
Have You?*

The Principle
of Purpose

_____

_____

_____

_____

_____

_____

_____

Draw a Mind Map like the one below of the people you should be talking to and working with on your current projects.

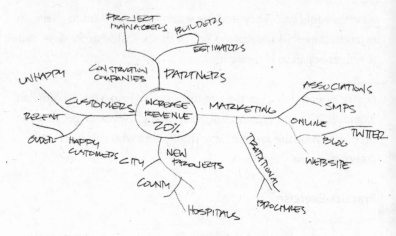

A Mind Map is a diagram used to represent words, ideas, tasks, or other items linked to and arranged around a central key word or goal.

To get good help, you have to give good help. Know what you have to offer the world and transact with it. Reach out and help people as much as possible. You will find reciprocity in favors owed back to you.

Live in generosity of character and notice how you will increase your ability to get help when you need it.

Remember that you will always need money to live the life of your dreams. We'll look at that topic more closely in the next part—the Principle of Prosperity.

44

Question One:

Have I talked to my personal team, family, friends etc that will support you fulfill on your commitments. List the people you should be talking to internally.

_____

_____

The Market
Has Changed
Have You?

The Principle
of Purpose

Question Two:

Have I spoken to enough of my existing customers to get a better understanding of their needs? List the customers you should be talking to.

_____

_____

Question Three:

Have I spoken to and enrolled my partners and vendors to support me? List the partners and vendors you should be talking to.

_____

_____

Use this information to draw yourself a mind map the lays out a network of powerful relationships to help you accomplish your goals.

Part 2

THE PRINCIPLE OF PROSPERITY

Step 6: KNOW YOUR PERSONAL NUMBERS

Step 7: KNOW YOUR BUSINESS NUMBERS

Step 8: KNOW YOUR MARKET NUMBERS

Step 9: NEGOTIATE POWERFULLY

Step 10: IT'S ALL ABOUT THE PROFIT

If you are like most salespeople, then you have probably spent some time daydreaming about money. What would it be like to have millions of dollars? What limitless possibilities that question opens up for us. We all have our own dreams of what we would do with a large amount of money. Some people would spend their days on the beach; others want to travel the world; and still others might want to underwrite the arts or support a charity. One thing is certain: We need money for everything—the house we live in, the food we eat, and the clothes we wear. Each day we are alive and breathing, we need money just to live. And your dreams, my friends, have a price tag, too.

- Do you know how much it costs you to live every day?
- How much money do you need this month? This year?
- Are you on track with your retirement plan?
- What are your benchmarks for success?
- How much money is enough for you to live your definition of a good life?

In a changing marketplace, we have to maintain our cash flow and bring in some revenue. During a recession, such as the one that started in 2008, the name of the game is to stay the course and survive the storm. If you're selling during a rapidly changing economy, your priority will be to survive; the heroics of swinging for the fences can come later.

In the **Wha-Dho** philosophy, the Principle of Prosperity requires you to align yourself with your numbers, so you are realistic with the resources you need to live a good life. Stay grounded in what these numbers mean—for you, for your company, and for your market segment.

How much money do you need? To get a good idea, answer the following questions:

- What are your dreams for the future?
- What is the purpose of your life?
- How much money do you need to fulfill these dreams of yours?

You may find it counterintuitive to approach the question of how much money you need this way. However, I urge you to follow this more logical approach. Second, know what you are committed to accomplishing in life. Then, have a good understanding about how much money is required to fulfill this commitment. Third, design powerful strategies and tactics to help you achieve it.

In addition, you will need other elements like enthusiasm, passion, insight, and determination to carry you through this tough or any other market. But, for now let us align your vision and commitment to succeed with real-world financial numbers that matter to you.

Step 6

KNOW YOUR PERSONAL NUMBERS

Know your financial numbers and what they mean. As revenue generators, we make money when we complete transactions with our customers. When times are good, we often assume that any success we experience might appropriately be our new baseline of activity. It's easy to become fooled by this form of success.

When times are good, most of us forget that markets go both ways—they go up and they go down. These cycles are part of the course and we need to plan for them, at a personal level as well as a business level.

A seasoned sales professional who sells technology for Oracle told me that the recession had prompted him to make changes in his life. His revenue targets had changed, and so did his income, but wanted to stay in sync with his future earnings. So, he sold his boat and started focusing on his three daughters, who would soon be heading to college. For him, that was a wise decision; he was paying attention to his personal numbers and managing his commitments. Most of us are aware that we need cash and resources to do the things we want to do and live the life we want to live. But do we really know how much money we need to live that lifestyle we want?As salespeople and revenue generators, we need to know what our revenue numbers mean to us at all times. It is in essence, management by the numbers—for yourself. Without money, we will be unable to live in our societies. As a result, we will be that much closer to pain and suffering. When looking at this idea through the lens of the **Wha-Dho** philosophy you must have a candid conversation with yourself about these matters. Before you can achieve prosperity, you must be aware of and committed to what you must accomplish:

- How much money do you need to live a good life?
- Do your collective salaries provide you this money?
- Is your strategy grounded in your vision?
- Are your revenue goals in sync with your market potential?
- Is your current marketplace static or changing?

If you answered any of these questions with "I don't know," then you need to plan a course of action you <u>do</u> know—one that will protect you in the long run and produce the results you need. You cannot reach a specific goal—such as living a prosperous life—without laying out your personal road map of success.

Once you know how much money you need, you will create the space to design, prepare to act, and then act powerfully.

Figure out how much money you need:

- How much money you currently have.
- How much money you need in the future.
- Calculate the gap between the two.

As a salesperson, you must be completely honest with yourself. If you are not achieving the revenue goals you set out for yourself, then you may not be making the income you need to live the life you want for yourself and your family. Look critically at this gap between the money you need to live your good life and your business and sales strategy to make the money you need.

Ask yourself:

- Will my current sales strategy yield the money I need?
- Is my market segment big enough?
- What changes do I have to make?

Because you picked up this book, you are probably experiencing a challenging sales environment. At this point, you might be struggling to meet your monthly revenue goals. You may also feel that your personal budget has come under significant strain. Let's see what needs to be done with it.

Start by creating a personal budget today. If you have one already, fantastic! Review it to make sure it is accurate and reflects the changes and the challenges you are experiencing in the market place. You must have numbers that reflect your reality.

Once you have established your personal budget, please get into the habit of reviewing it on a regular basis. You need to really understand how much money you have at any given time and how much more you need to fulfill your commitments.

- Do you need a better strategy plan?
- Do you need more training?
- Do you need a better product to sell?

If they are real, if they are accurate, numbers do not lie. Work your numbers; learn to speak the language of numbers, and get comfortable around them. Everything in business is related to dollars and cents—and you need to be comfortable with them.

Practice Exercise

Are you working with a personal monthly or yearly budget? If not, create one with either an Excel spreadsheet or a notebook. Once you have a yearly or annual budget, you can start calculating how much money you will need for your living expenses as well as your retirement.

Sample Budget for Monthly Expenses

Mortgage or Rent	$
Utilities	$
Transportation	$
Insurances	$
Taxes	$
Food	$
Clothing	$
Travel	$
Medical Expenses	$
Entertainment and Dining	$
Home Improvement	$
Retirement Savings	$
Other Savings (i.e. College Fund)	$
Financial Reserves	$
Other (i.e. Tithing, Hobbies)	$
Total	$

Now, do the same thing for your revenue sources. There is nothing complex here, just simple listing and addition—but it is seeing it in writing that makes it powerful.

My Salary	$
My Commission	$
Investment Income	$
Other Income	$
Total	$

The next calculation is for additional income.

Sample Budget for Calculating Needed Additional Income

a. Five-Year Savings Goals	$
b. Current Savings	$
Additional Income Needed	a – b ÷ 60

This is a simple task, but it can be daunting and leave you discouraged. Please don't let that stop you from doing it, though.

Resources

A good resource for helping you with budgeting and financial planning is http://www.uncommonwaytowealth.com/

Step 7

*The Market
Has Changed
Have You?*

Paul D'Souza

When a marketplace changes, the cost of goods and services also changes. Some items and services become quite costly, while other prices tumble dramatically. When you are selling in a changing sales environment, your standard profitability model can quickly become outdated.

- The cost of your raw materials may increase in price.
- Your vendors may charge less to stay competitive.
- Your competitors may lower their prices.
- Your competitors may also offer sales incentives that you must match to keep your customers.
- Long-term, established customers may suffer budget cutbacks and want better payment terms.

In a changing sales environment, things change fast. Last week's prices may have become completely uncompetitive. Or, your selling prices may have become unprofitable, because your cost of goods might have gone up.

Case in Point

In February 2009, I spoke with Neil Wadhawan, the CEO of Heartwood Studios, which produces custom 3D training simulations. His market had changed in sudden and dramatic ways. Neil's customers saw their budgets slashed. Most projects were put on hold, except those that were already critical. As a result, his business numbers changed almost overnight.

54

Neil was shocked when he realized his monthly expenses had increased 25% in one month in relation to his revenue number. He had to restructure Heartwood and its budget to get in sync with the drastically changed market. He quickly restructured working relationships with people. Some key employees became independent contractors, and others were let go. Not pleasant, but a realistic response to the market. The end result: Heartwood is still around, and doing well:

When a marketplace changes, you have to reexamine all of your financial assumptions. You must look at your numbers in detail.

- Know what revenue you can count on.
- Know what your expenses are.
- Plan how to do more with less.

When you know your business numbers and monitor them, you can actively and appropriately respond to market changes before or as they occur—not after. If you don't know your numbers, you and your business will react to the market, instead of proceeding proactively. Your company's belated responses may come too late to avoid substantial losses, and you may miss significant opportunities for substantial gains in revenue and profit.

Manage your sales activity by the numbers. Sales managers know what their projections are, and sales reps have quotas to maintain. So, look to your numbers for guidance when you decide how to move in a changing market. Manage the balance between the short-term and long-term deals. Pay attention to the deals that will make the most difference in winning future business, and leave the long-shots for a more favorable business environment.

In May 2009, I was at a town hall meeting with the Greater Cincinnati Venture Association. One of the panelists, Mark Richey of Draper Triangle Ventures, said they were going back to each one of their 73 portfolio companies to redo their projections for the rest of the year and help them align with the market.

Do that with your entire book of business.

Case in Point

Nonprofits also need to know their business numbers. Leyton Cougar, the executive director of the Wild Spirit Wolf Sanctuary in Ramah, New Mexico, pays close attention to the wholesale cost of chicken; it is, of course, food for the wolves. At one point, the price jumped from eighteen cents per pound to nearly ninety cents per pound. You can imagine what an impact that must have had on his budget.

Leyton's business, which feeds and protects wolves, is a nonprofit— but it still needs to follow the basic rules of business. Though his passion to care for wolves does not require him to make a profit, he does need income, in the form of donations, to cover his expenses.

Each day, Leyton makes a continuous stream of sales calls. He describes these as fund-raising calls, but they are sales calls all the same. Leyton enlists people to give him money to support the wolves; instead of selling a product or a service, he sells a cause. He still has, however, operating expenses and everything else that goes along with running a business. When the price of chicken increases fivefold, he faces a tough choice. Either he needs more money to feed his wolves chicken or he needs to find a cheaper food.

Leyton notes: "When I started doing this seven years ago, we were working with a $50,000 annual budget. The calls to save wolves kept coming in, and the business needed more money to meet this urgent demand—simple as that. So, I brought professionalism to what we were doing, while increasing our scope and involvement with the community. I started going out, giving talks anywhere I could, in schools, at county fairs, and on radio and television shows, and I took my wolves with me. We got the Web site up, took videos and photographs, and started making phone calls. Thank God people have responded. We now work with a $400,000 annual budget and yet, there is more to do."

So you see it doesn't matter if it is a company or a nonprofit organization. Your numbers must align or the enterprise will not survive.

See more of Leyton Cougar at http://www.wildspiritwolfsanctuary.org

Practice Exercise

When a sales environment changes, you often have to rebalance your priorities, ask yourself some tough questions, and make hard (but necessary) choices. When you feel as if you are fighting financial fires, it is time to focus on the immediate short- and midterm opportunities. What does your sales budget look like for this month, this quarter, and the rest of this year?

Sample Budget

Use this approach to monitor the deals in your pipeline. You can specify the timeline.

Customer Name	Likeli-hood of Sale (%)	Revenue Value	Estimate Value	**Commis-sion = 5% Value**
Roberts	90%	$10,000	$9,000	$450.00
Jane Doe	50%	$10,000	$5,000	$250.00
John Doe	10%	$10,000	$1,000	$50.00
Total		**$30,000**	**$16,000**	**$750.00**

Knowing these business numbers will help you plan, operate, and manage yourself and your business to compete successfully in the marketplace.

- You will have an accurate sense of where to focus your efforts.
- You will know where your short-term deals are.
- You will know which deals to drop.

Knowing your company's numbers and where your deals are coming from is not enough when working through a tough market. To make sure you hit your revenue targets as planned and budgeted, you will also need to know how the market is doing. There are too many moving parts and changing variables that can alter your bottom line; you will need to know your market's numbers—the next step.

Step 8

KNOW YOUR MARKET NUMBERS

Markets appear and markets disappear because of the million moving parts that can affect them—from changes in technology to wars in foreign lands, to political and demographic changes here at home, to name just a few. It is important to follow the market's pulse and react quickly. If you are exceptionally attentive, you can even anticipate the change by interpreting the signs. When Hurricane Katrina hit New Orleans, it had a ripple effect on the markets. In many places, the cost of gasoline skyrocketed from $1.50 a gallon to $3.30 a gallon in a day. This dramatic change hit suddenly and affected business everywhere across the United States. In a changing market, pay close attention to what has changed and the financial impact these changes could have on your business. I am talking about the real numbers that influence your market segment.

The Market Has Changed Have You?

The Principle of Prosperity

- What are your cost-of-goods and other operating expenses?
- What are your customers willing to pay for your services?
- How do these numbers affect your profit margin?

In a tough market, these numbers can change quickly and without warning. During tough economic conditions, demand is usually down, and customers want bigger discounts for lower volume sales orders. This might just be your new reality. But reality it is—and you need to adjust to meet it.

Case in Point

Consider the story of Susan Horner, a real estate agent in Ohio, who has managed to stay very busy selling homes throughout this tough market. She did it by refocusing her sales efforts. Previously, most of her sales were homes between $300,000 and $500,000. To Susan's credit, she changed when the market did. In these tough times, she is selling multiple homes each month in the sub $250,000 range. In adapting to a new baseline reality, she successfully read the market and followed its numbers.

The Market Has Changed Have You?

Paul D'Souza

At any given time, there could be several factors that affect the cost of goods and services in your market segment:

- Financial dynamics and credit problems.
- Advancements in technology.
- Demographic changes that skew demand.
- Political and compliance issues.

When the price of gas went up, the market's need for gas guzzlers like the Hummer changed: it disappeared. Instead, customers bought the more cost-effective and "smart cars" like the Toyota Prius and the Ford Focus. Companies that did not foresee these trends lost market share. The market is indifferent to you and your interests; it will chart its own course regardless of you and your efforts. When you recognize that your market has changed, communicate with others more than you normally would. You cannot afford to be left out of the conversation when change happens. When you are talking with your customers, partners, and vendors, find out:

- Has the cost of goods changed?
- Who is paying for what?
- How much are customers paying?
- What is in demand?
- Where is the supply coming from?
- How strong are your customers?

Be attentive to your market's numbers to help you solve problems, manage your risks, and take advantage of opportunities.

Practice Exercises

Consider doing what we call the Selling by Survey technique. Call your customers and find out what problems they are facing—specifically, how has the market changed and altered their costs of doing business? List five customers you will contact in the next week:

1. _____

2. _____

3. _____

4. _____

5. _____

Ask each the following questions:

- What are the core changes in your market?
- How are these changes affecting your businesses?
- What business problems do you need help with?
- What will it take to win your business?

Once you know what their issues are, you will begin to connect the dots and have a better understanding of what is going on in your market segment. You will be in better position to give customers powerful and accurate solutions to the problems they have.

Step 9

NEGOTIATE POWERFULLY

Everyone usually wants a deal. Good businesspeople, on the other hand, know that more often than not, you get what you pay for and smart businesspeople will not try to squeeze you past a certain point. In a changing market, when everyone feels pressure from uncertainty, deal negotiations for a better price can go to extreme levels. You will see this pattern happen at all sizes of businesses and organizations, from the largest corporations to individual buyers.

The Market Has Changed Have You?

The Principle of Prosperity

In December 2008, I was at Cisco's headquarters working through a deal. The people from Cisco did not ask for a handout, but they asked for numbers that would fit their budgets. They did it in a way that included the benefits of our partnering with them, because our offers complemented their products and services. They were willing to get us on their approved vendor list and give us access to a channel of customers, in return for a discount on the services they were buying from us. They were conserving their cash resources in a tough, changing market, but they were also opening other doors for us. This leadership showed us Cisco's business professionalism and maturity, and I respected them for it.

In a changing market, you can expect every customer to look for ways to spend less money with you. You will have many conversations where the customer wants to delay a contract or reduce the costs. Do not get discouraged. When you hear people negotiating seriously over price, you should instead be optimistic; you likely are hearing a very strong buying signal from your prospect.

These conversations will happen. So be prepared with a few different pricing models ready to share with your customers. But, please make sure you protect yourself. Do not negotiate in a way that is not beneficial to you and your business. A good negotiation process has to go both ways; both parties have to see value in the structure of the working relationship. Creatively share value, and work so that both parties experience value.

Understanding Total Cost of Ownership

It also helps to understand the difference between cost vs. price when negotiating with your customers. Because your customers are usually going to be looking at their Total Cost of Ownership, I believe it is critical for all of us in the business of generating revenue to have a good understanding of this concept.

Let me explain. You offer your customers a new business application at a very good price. You offer the best price they have seen, and they like it. But then they discover that your solution comes with certain costs:

- It requires them to invest in staff training.
- It requires more supervision.
- It requires computer upgrades.

In this example, the sales price was right, but the costs associated with purchasing your application might have been too high to bear at this time.

Consider all factors that go into the total cost of ownership when you help you customers assess value and their return on investment (ROI) when considering what you have to sell them. In a sense, walk in their shoes and take their interests to heart. They will appreciate your efforts and increase their trust in you. In tough markets, this is all the more necessary and important.

One common negotiating tactic people use is asserting that you stand to win more business after they sign a deal with you. In effect what they want you to do is give them a high volume discount, for their initial order. This sounds fine as a conversation, but on these terms there can be no guarantees. (If your exposure to risk and lost revenue can tolerate this kind of uncertainty, this approach works well, as it did for me at Cisco.)

I suggest that you do not buy into this hypothetical upfront cost with a future benefit if it presents too much risk for you. Perhaps you can build performance-based incentives into a working relationship with your customer. Be creative, and even consider trading resources if necessary. Do not ignore the fundamentals of business and economics when talking about the initial deal in these circumstances. Be clear on the merits and the value of the deal for both parties. Please also resist offering your customers more value than is necessary. This usually has a negative result, by diluting the value of services or product already offered.

I would suggest that only once your initial deal is complete and you have developed a good working relationship with your customer, you can and should you consider selling more product or services to that same account or group of people.

Remember these key points:

- No deal is better than a bad deal.
- Make a profit, not just revenue.
- Try to negotiate on options, not price.

Practice Exercise

Learn to negotiate a win-win deal that makes your customers appreciate the value they feel they received in dealing with you. Remember—it's not always about the money; people experience value in many ways. Look for impact and other benefits they will experience.

One negotiating technique that is used very often and in many situations is the "Three-Part Response" to customer comments and questions. Here is a possible scenario:

Customer:
How much does your solution cost? *Your response:*

Part One
I do not know your specifics, as every customer has different needs and requirements. Can you please tell me more about what you are looking for?

The customer does this, giving you more information to make your case and more opportunities to build rapport and trust.

Part Two
We have found that customers with similar needs have spent anywhere between $X and $Y on their solutions.

This response shows them that your solution can be configured in several ways, giving them the ability to customize a solution to fit both their needs and their budget. In essence, you have added value.

Part Three
Does this price range fit with your budget?

Here is a planning tool you can use to prepare your talking and negotiation points. It provides a helpful visual model of what all the potential situations might be.

Things You Want	Things They Want
Higher price; cash up-front; high volume; large projects or orders	Low cost; low-volume commitment; good payment terms; small projects
Fears You Might Have	**Fears They Might Have**
budget limits; support needs; unrealistic customer expectations	Price; reputation; capabilities; support

The above grid will help you plan and be prepared for most questions or requests that customers might have for you. Do research on customers and their business so you can anticipate what they are thinking. Know what is important to them. Go prepared with several packages and options they can choose from. This will help them find the right solution that meets both their business requirements and their budget. Always negotiate on options—i.e., features, functions, service plans—rather than negotiating on price.

Negotiate on options as much as possible and do not drop your price without getting something in return for it.

Resources

Negotiating Skills with Brian Dietmeyer, President and CEO of Think! Inc. Video interview at www.sellingpower.com

Step 10

*The Market
Has Changed
Have You?*

Paul D'Souza

It's always about the profit. In a recent conversation with Neil Rackham, the author of *SPIN Selling,* he mentioned how CEOs across the world are now focusing on making their revenue numbers from good, profitable business. They have become more efficient in their operations, which was the trend 15 to 20 years ago. Over the last 10 years or so, it was accessing growth through acquisitions and mergers. Now it's all about old-fashioned growth, which comes from profitable sales and growing market penetration and footprint.

When business becomes difficult, and you are navigating through troubled waters, you often forget to savor small successes. I've seen plenty of salespeople become so focused on making the big sales—bringing in that big fish—that they forget to work on the smaller deals that could close easily and very often bring in higher profit margins.

Large revenue without profit may not be as valuable as less revenue with a healthy profit margin. For many years, Jerry Hobbs worked for Horton Homes, the Georia manufacturer of mobile and modular homes. He recently began selling real estate. Near the end of his first year, he was on track to do a million dollars in booked business—and he was doing it by helping customers buy homes in the $150,000 to $200,000 range. Many of his colleagues were not doing so well; they were chasing the big fish, the $600,000 lakefront properties, a tougher sale in a shrinking market. Jerry is still selling real estate, helping people moving into a good home.

68

Over the last 25 years, I have worked with many people in business. In that time, I have seen people focus exclusively on top-line revenue without ensuring that the profit margins are protected. This hurts business, plain and simple. Essentially, they often wind up working for free. When you add in overhead costs and lost-opportunity costs, they may even be spending more money than they receive from their customers on some of their deals. This is not a good way of doing things.

Business organizations exist to first survive and then to make a profit. Without cash flow and profits, a business quickly withers away and dies. A company, when it becomes a mature organization, also needs profits to fulfill its mission. Usually, a company's profit is directly related to giving its owners and stockholders a bigger return on their investment. Yet at other companies, it might be something else. One such company is Newman's Own. Here is the message from its Web site:

> Newman's Own Foundation continues Paul Newman's commitment to donate all profits to charity. Over $265 million has been given to thousands of charities since 1982. Learn more about our mission at www.newmansownfoundation.org.

Notice the company's statement that it would donate "all profits" to charity. Without profits, it could not be fulfilling on its mission, which is to offer support to the many charities they support. They need profits to fulfill their mission.

Profit sometimes comes in unexpected ways. Mr. Roberts, the owner of a business called Full of Goodness that sells gift items at wholesale prices to retailers, says:

For me right now, small is the new big. In my former corporate life, in various roles, I managed from 30 to 160 people. When I left that life to start my own company, I had 5 employees. Little by little, through attrition, I shrunk. When they left, I never replaced them. I kept that profit to myself. As each one left, the moneys that would have gone into paying them went instead to inventory. In my case, my larger inventory generated greater sales growth and more profit for me. Now, I'm the only employee. If I have a super busy show, I contract a few people who will help me work my booth. I work seven days a week, 12-20 hours a day. And I love what I do. I have no stress. I run a company that is free of artifice and pretense. And, best of all, I will never retire. Even if we move back to Alabama someday, I can still do what I do. So, my sales have grown for 10 consecutive years. My profits have grown as well. Keep in mind, again, that 80% of my sales are in Michigan—supposedly ravaged by the decline of the auto manufacturers and the recession.

The Market Has Changed Have You?

Paul D'Souza

Mr. Roberts understands that more employees will not guarantee growth or profit for him, so he made business decisions that helped him make more profit.

Your situation may be different; you may need many employees in your company to achieve success. However, you should know which factors produce the greatest positive impact on your company's profitability. If all of a business's revenues go toward paying expenses and operating costs, then the business will not be able to take advantage of a good market and expand—nor will it have the cash reserves necessary to keep going during a difficult sales environment. What makes a business sustainable is its ability to make a profit, which is then utilized for the growth of the business, and its ability to survive and redesign or restructure itself in a down market.

Practice Exercise

Review the products and services that you and your company sell to learn whether you are selling them at a profit. If you do not have access to the numbers, then speak to someone who can help you understand your break-even price points and profit margins. Do the following for each product or service.

Base Product	$
Marketing Costs	$
Break-Even Point	$
Ideal Sale Price	$

Far too often, I come across people who are so focused on making a sale that they forget their fundamental need to make a profit. Never mistake cash flow for profit. They are two different things, and if you believe that cash flow will inherently include profit, then your hard work might just be in vain. When you give profit the attention it deserves, you are committing to do whatever it takes to realize a profit. Make deals with customers who value what you do and who pay you enough money to make a significant profit.

To achieve this goal, you might have to alter what you sell and who you sell it to. In other words, you might need new customers and a new sales process. We will examine this issue in the third part of the **Wha-Dho** philosophy—the Principle of Process.

Part 3

THE PRINCIPLE OF PROCESS

Step 11: REDEFINE YOURSELF

Step 12: REDESIGN YOUR OFFER

Step 13: QUALIFY OPPORTUNITIES FAST

Step 14: MAKE POWERFUL OFFERS

Step 15: SELL SOMETHING OF VALUE

Before you begin reading this part, I hope you take the time to review the first two parts of the **Wha-Dho** sales philosophy—the Principle of Purpose and the Principle of Prosperity. This will reinforce your purpose and help you specify how much money you need to accomplish it. In this part of **Wha-Dho**, you will design the best process (strategy and tactics) to help you achieve your desired results.

To begin the process, you need to ask yourself these questions:

- What is my strategy to be successful?
- What new tactics must I take to win?

Throughout my career, I have noticed that most people do not make the effort to consider these questions seriously. Instead, a lot of people go through the motions day in and day out: working a job, taking care of their families, and "hoping" it will all work out in the end. This is not powerful. As salespeople and business owners, they work hard, some even work smart—yet, most often they live paycheck to paycheck. Unfortunately, the market is indifferent to what people want and the only thing we can do is design a better strategy for our careers, one that will yield results.

The market has changed—have you? We need to work in ways that yield results *today*. This is the time for creativity and insight.

I was talking to Ellia Kassoff of Strategic Software Resources and he reported having a blockbuster year, now in 2009! He says his success is directly related to his sales strategy and how he works with his customers to solve their human resources problems and needs. Other recruiters usually call customers and just ask if they have any openings to fill.

Please do not live your life on autopilot. If you are young and in the early stages of your career, do not start this unhealthy habit. If you feel trapped in a routine, if you have heard yourself say "same old, same old" to a friend when they ask you how things are going—Wake up! shake out of your rut, and chart a new course of action.

Ask yourself:

- Have I been making "robocalls" my entire working life? Selling the same thing in the same way?
- Do I keep going back to the same dry wells—and then complain about not finding water?
- Do I ever wonder why others are succeeding, but not me?

To live the life you want to live, to be fulfilled, you have to know where you are going, and you have to do things that support reaching your goals. It's time to take responsibility and chart your own course to success.

As a salesperson with a revenue number, you want to make sure you talk to well-qualified prospects who have an interest in what you have to offer. Then, you have to get them to buy something—i.e., take action and agree to give you money. Your company makes money, and you get paid. In essence, this is the whole point. Nothing else matters.

- Why do anything that is counterproductive to achieving your ultimate purpose?
- Are you focusing on actions powerful enough to produce the results you seek?

Your daily actions (your process) must support both your purpose and your financial goals. When you focus on your process, you will move closer toward your ultimate goal—your purpose; doing any other tasks or actions will end up being counterproductive. Remember, if you take the wrong actions, you will incur opportunity costs in the future as well as hard costs in the present.

In this part, we will discuss how to design and build powerful offers and sales strategies to generate the money needed to pursue the dreams you want to live.

The Market Has Changed Have You?

The Principle of Process

Step 11

The Market Has Changed Have You?

Paul D'Souza

In tough selling environments and changing markets, companies and salespeople make a critical mistake. They do what they do best—they sell their favorite solutions, products, and services. When cash becomes tight, salespeople and marketers beat their drums louder and proudly announce their newest offers, but the market pays little attention, unless it is what their customers can immediately use to solve real problems. The problem is that you are doing the same old, same old again.

In changing markets, you need to design your go-to-market strategies around solving the business problems your customers want to solve rather than offering them your coolest solutions to problems they might not have or want to solve. Customers will spend money when they can solve problems that are important to them. This means you need to align with your customers and help them make more money or reduce their risks in a changing market.

What can you do for your customers to help them increase revenue today? Here is a list of possibilities:

- Focus on solving your customers' problems.
- Find out how you can help your customers now.
- Be creative and innovative at every step.
- Use sales strategies your customers appreciate.
- Network with people who can help you.
- Strengthen your entire network of relationships.

- Remember to ask for the order, for business.
- When appropriate, ask for referrals.

Make success your goal. Be totally willing to restructure yourself and your business activity to meet the market's new conditions. Embrace change so that you can meet your customers' needs.

Case in Point

A few years ago, I was selling an IT solution to the medical-communications departments of pharmaceutical companies, both large and small. Our prospects had been paying $70,000 for a solution to a problem. We then showed up with a much better application, which happened to cost anywhere between $1.2 and $4.3 million; it was a very different application with a very different price point.

To avoid competition based on price, we decided to move away from competing with technology against technology, and focused our entire presentation on the business value of helping our customers reduce their risk of being fined for noncompliance by the Federal Drug Administration (FDA).

This strategy turned out to be a wise decision; fines levied by the FDA can be enormous. Normally, when people think of fines, they might think of a traffic ticket that costs them a couple hundred dollars. But when the FDA fines a pharmaceutical manufacturer, it can be truly massive. In 2000, for example, Schering Plough was fined $500 million by the FDA. No person wants to be responsible for a $500 million fine.

Our solution was well received, because we used existing technology our customers already had in house, and we customized it to solve problems customers were currently dealing with. I will never forget how one of our customers presented its deployment of our solution at a national conference and told peers what a wonderful job we did. The customer also suggested people stop by our booth and schedule a demo of the application to see for themselves. My sales partner, Ben Harris, and I made 18 presentations in 2½ days and booked close to $9.3 million in revenue over a three-year period.

Practice Exercise

Anchor yourself in your commitment to succeed. Get creative about how you go about increasing revenue. Your markets might have changed, but believe that you are still the powerhouse of potential and capability you have always been. You are a problem-solver, a person with a wide network of friends and resources in the community. You are still someone who wins.Here are some questions to ask yourself:

What keeps my customers up at night? Can I reconfigure our solutions to solve those problems?

_____

_____

_____

_____

Where can I begin to solve problems for my customers today?

_____

_____

_____

Can I enter a new business area that would be valuable to my customers?

_____

_____

_____

Where do I need help and whom can I call on to ask for that help?

_____

_____

_____

You should reflect on these answers yourself, but you might also ask your peers and colleagues to help you brainstorm questions like these. I encourage you to even reach out to your customers and ask them about how their needs align with what you do. You may be surprised by their responses.

Step 12

REDESIGN YOUR OFFER

The Market Has Changed Have You?

Paul D'Souza

Your customers have changed. The Internet gives them the ability to do research and find the best deal in the comfort of their own offices and homes, and at times convenient for them.

Customers' ability to shop around, compare prices and service, and get the best deal inhibits your ability to create a sense of urgency. They control the power at all times. When they meet with you, they may be gathering information or be equipped with information from your competitors' Web sites.

In general, customers now have higher expectations about the responsiveness and professionalism they want in business. They no longer want to wait a day or two for an answer. They want immediate feedback.

The process of buying and the marketplace have changed; your customers' needs have evolved. Have you changed?

Put yourself in your customers' shoes for a moment. Technology has changed their expectations. Take, for instance, how Dell and Amazon inform people about the status of their orders. Or think about all the things we can do on these new Web 2.0 sites.

Case in Point

One of my colleagues, Chris Derry, had an interesting experience

80

back in 2003, when he committed himself to starting a state-based think tank, Bluegrass Institute, in his home state of Kentucky. Chris took on the challenge of trying to explain why the principles of liberty, free markets, and limited government were good ideas to hold on to, especially relevant in our current economic condition, and worthy of forming the ideological foundation of state and local public policy.

The Market Has Changed Have You?

The Principle of Process

When doing market research for this project, Chris was surprised to learn that his potential customers were more interested in combating corruption and other ills in their government than in establishing governmental policy.

So Chris faced two options: deal with a roadblock to his original idea or embrace the new opportunity. The fundamentals of salesmanship were in play. It was time to redesign his offer and come up with a solution addressed the interests of potential customers, the residents of the commonwealth of Kentucky.

Chris designed a powerful offer that would:

- Leverage the Internet.
- Embrace social networking.
- Provide visibility into government records.
- Allow the community to contribute.
- Increase utilization by permitting anonymous participation.

When Chris proposed this idea to potential contributors, the funding for his think tank increased by 50% the following year. He listened carefully to his customers, and then he personalized his offer to meet their needs. In addition, he leveraged the Internet and other forms of technology that his customers were familiar with; giving them the ability to participate and make a difference.

Review your offer and your sales approach.

- Do you need to redesign your offer?
- Is your offer relevant today?
- Is your offer valuable today?
- Are you using web-based technologies?
- Are your customers' needs being met?

You lose credibility any time you sell something of low or—even worse—no value to a customer. You may be eager to make a sale in this tough market, but I would urge you to make the right sales. Offering your customers products and service they do not see as valuable will hurt your credibility. Seth Godin, bestselling author, entrepreneur, and agent of change, notes that when customers see you suffering, they stay away. Fire sales and deep discounts will erode your company's brand and perceived value over the long term.

Take the lead in changing times. Assess the value of your product or service and redesign it if necessary.

Understand value: Value is an assessment that something is worthwhile and important. The solution you offer your customers must be worth the time, money, resources, and lost opportunities associated with acquiring it. Is your offer valuable to your prospects?

Leverage Sales 2.0 technologies and social media: Sales 2.0 technologies help you increase, improve on, and manage your customer interactions and engagements. Maximize your ability to communicate with your target prospects and customers. There are many new Sales 2.0 technologies that can support you in communicating with your customer in very powerful ways.

Resources

You might improve your sales ratios by leveraging some of these technologies in your sales process.

www.eloqua.com—Lead management and sales enablement.

www.genius.com—Real-time marketing automation.

www.landslide.com—Sales process management.

www.sales2.com—The Sales 2.0 Services Company.

Social media—such as Twitter, YouTube, FaceBook, and LinkedIn—are sites where a lot of your customers are spending time. You might want to be there too. Each site has its own protocol and style. Learn the etiquette of the social media channel you choose to leverage and be part of to be successfull in accessing your customers there.

Technology will not stand still; it will change and so must you. It will continue to advance and provide new ways for you to interact with your customers. This reminds me of the phrase "Follow the herd." You must go where your customers are.

As you seek to redesign your offer to the market and solve customers' problems, ask yourself these questions:

- What do my customers need today?
- How can I help them?
- How do I position and market the idea?

You can leverage your existing relationships, have powerful conversations, and design new offers to help your customers cope with these challenging times. They will appreciate it and reward you for it by doing business with you.

Practice Exercise

Noticing the needs people have creates the space for you to make a sale.

Call three of your best customers today and talk to them about their business. Find out:

1. Is your offer relevant to them?
2. Do you need to change anything?

_____

_____

_____

_____

_____

_____

Call three of your business partners and talk to them about the state of their business. Ask them:

1. What trends are they noticing?
2. What technologies are they using?

_____

_____

_____

_____

_____

_____

Attend three networking events with your industry in the next 30 days.

_____

_____

_____

Step 13

QUALIFY OPPORTUNITIES FAST

---

*The Market
Has Changed
Have You?*

Paul D'Souza

In a changing marketplace, you must know how to accelerate the velocity of your deals. When the marketplace changes, the sales cycle will stretch and get longer. You must counteract this trend and close deals faster. If you do not pay attention to the process, then you will spend a lot of energy chasing rabbits (unlikely business). In a changing marketplace, your prospects may not know what solution they need, or they may merely be exploring new options without the intent to buy anything in the near future. You must qualify your customers and all your business opportunities as fast as possible. If you do this well, you will be rewarded financially and have peace of mind, knowing that you are engaged in "real" business that could lead to a sale. Some people describe this as identifying the "no" prospects quickly, so that you can spend more time with the customers that say yes.

In my experience, I believe that a prospect is qualified to transact when the following conditions are present:

1. They have a problem that needs to be fixed.
2. An assigned budget.
3. Trust in you, the vendor.
4. Clear timelines for action.
5. There are bad consequences for no action.

Very often, I find salespeople working with prospects they have not qualified well. This can be frustrating and costly.

86

Case in Point

Denis Clark is an ex-IBM'er who had a billion-dollar sales quota as vice president of sales and marketing in IBM's Software Division. He is now the EVP of sales for a start-up company that has a potential customer base of approximately 1900 prospects.

The sales team had been focused on a very small percentage of that pool—less than 10%. One of the campaigns Denis launched was to have his team of sales associates get through as many of the 1900 prospects as possible. He tells his team: "Quickly get through those people who say No, and only work with the people who get what we do, and say Yes."

The turnaround has been significant with growth in revenues every month in these tough markets of 2009. The take away from this story is: Don't spend your time trying to convert the people who are saying 'No'. Spend your time identifying and working with people who say 'Yes' to what you have to offer them. When you have exhausted the Yes's then go back and convert the No's.

Some salespeople take shortcuts and qualify their prospects only partially. They become impatient because they believe they have a shot at a deal. This is not effective. Move on!

Here are some guidelines to help you qualify your customers and the sales opportunities they present to you.

- Do your research—you have to be an expert in their business.
- Know the value of the opportunities.
- Learn to ask tough business questions.
- Build rapport and trust.

- Always stay on track; talk only about issues that will move your deal forward.

Case in Point

The Market Has Changed Have You?

Paul D'Souza

A few years ago, I was working on an opportunity to sell an IT solution to Ortho Bio-Tech, a Johnson & Johnson company. My contact there, the director of Information Systems, was interested in what we had to offer, integrating Siebel and Documentum, two large computer applications for the enterprise. But, because of other corporate initiatives, the project we were discussing was put on hold.

The customer was interested, but there would be no deal now. So, I moved to focus on other opportunities, which was a more promising and potentially more lucrative way to spend my time.

The delay took the pressure off our communication and allowed us to talk about other things. I found something I could help him with. He needed help with standardizing Ortho's content management environment. We were very good at that kind of work and won a $400,000 project we did not know existed.

Practice Exercise

In order to qualify leads, you must perfect your ability to ask leading questions. Simultaneously, you must notice the elements needed to close the deal.

Taking the top 3 deals in your pipeline, go through this list for each:

1. Has the prospect clearly identified a business need?

_____

_____

2. Do you have rapport and trust with the prospect?

_____

_____

3. Does the prospect have an approved budget?

_____

_____

4. Are there clear timelines in which the prospect needs to act?

_____

_____

5. Are there bad consequences if the prospect doesn't act?

_____

_____

Step 14

MAKE POWERFUL OFFERS

The Market Has Changed Have You?

Paul D'Souza

If you want to complete highly valued transactions, then you must make powerful offers to the marketplace. Highly valued transactions provide you, the salesperson, with the best return on your investments of time, energy, and money, while providing your customers with a solution that is valuable and worth their investments of time, money, and effort they make in you; in brief, these transactions are assessed as valuable to both you and your customers. We all want more of these deals!

When the market conditions change, so should you and what you sell. Stay in sync with your customers at all times. Offer solutions to business problems they have. They need your help—go make a difference in their lives.

Make powerful offers that help your customers:

1. Solve real problems.
2. Reduce risk.
3. Save or make money.

Case in Point

Mark Faust, the founder of the consulting firm Echelon Management, was working with a vice president of a Fortune 500 company on a sales training he was going to do for about 100 sales executives in a specific division. Mark had customized a whole series of

90

exercises for a full eight-hour training session. The VP was excited, because Mark had made him a powerful offer and shown him how he was going to address some significant issues that he believed was holding the team back from producing greater results. We are talking a seven-figure increase to their annual sales goal—no small change! At the same time, the president of the company sent out a message to his VPs mandating that "all training sessions be canceled" for budget reasons, including the one Mark was to do.

It was only because Mark had made the VP a powerful offer, helping him address real problems and doing what was necessary with his sales team to make more money, that the VP had no problem standing up to his president and getting his meeting. He trained his staff and they produced the results he set out to accomplish.

I love this story, because this is exactly what we as salespeople need to be doing. We need to get into our customers' lives and solve real problems for them.

When we follow good business practices and help people solve problems, we help them get more out of life. This is why I am in sales, and why am proud to be a sales professional.

Here are three guidelines you can use to work through your powerful offers;

1. Get your customers involved in your sales process; increased participation usually increases perceived value. This will make it easier to secure critical information needed to help you produce exceptional results for them.
2. Try to get paid up front, at least with a partial payment. This will help your customers increase their commitment

to you financially as well as in their attention and with other resources.

3. Quantify the incremental value that your customers will realize by implementing your solution. Let them take the lead in defining these benchmarks of success.

Practice Exercise

Pick five customers you have a good working relationship with and list them below.

1. _____

2. _____

3. _____

4. _____

5. _____

Call them, or better still, meet them and ask them these questions. The questions will help you get the information needed to design a powerful new offer that is valuable to them and profitable to you.

1. Would you give me two or three examples of things I could do that would make our solution more valuable and useful to you?

2. What problems are you trying to solve now?

3. What are your strategic initiatives through the next 12 months?

92

Step 15

SELL SOMETHING OF VALUE

My four-year-old nephew recently taught me a valuable lesson. My wife and I were visiting family and in a happy mood I gave my wife a hug and very dramatically announced how much I loved her. What I heard next was a lesson in the fundamentals of sales and marketing—and may I add totally unexpected, especially from a 4-year-old. Without taking his eyes off the TV, he said in a matter-of-fact tone, "Who cares!" Seth Godin, the world's leading marketing guru, says the same thing: "Customers don't care about you."

Imagine yourself meeting with your customers. You outline your latest product or solution. You discuss the features and benefits at length. But did you ask them what they are looking for or what they are interested in? It is always about them, and what they think is valuable—not what you think is valuable.

You can only capture and retain listeners' attention when you talk about topics that have value to them. When people receive your offers, they review everything you are saying through their own filters of interest. They will see and hear things that are important to them. They cannot do otherwise, because their filters of comprehension and understanding are always tuned to taking care of their own concerns—not yours.

As a salesperson, a businessperson, and someone committed to a revenue number, you must sell something for a profit. So, the fastest way to make a sale and increase revenue is to:

The Market Has Changed Have You?

The Principle of Process

- Sell something your customers need.
- Solve a problem they have.
- Help them save or make more money.

Case in Point

The Market Has Changed Have You?

Paul D'Souza

I was recently working with the owner of an upscale Middle Eastern restaurant in the Midwest. He had heard about what I do and asked for some help. What got my attention was a comment he made the first time we met. He said, "I have tried everything I know! Nothing is working." The restaurant was operating at 50% capacity; he was losing money.

I asked the owner a few leading questions that related to specific demographic segments of his guests:

- How many guests were Middle Eastern?
- How many were from the local community?
- How often did the regulars come in?

Unfortunately, he did not have most of these numbers.

The solutions we talked about were simple, but they centered on the owner redesigning his core offering to meet the demand and the interests of his local customers. He got away from his vision of what he started with and started selling food that his customers wanted; he got busy and he started making money.

As salespeople, we often get excited about what we have to offer our customers, but without much consideration for our customers' interests. This is a bad idea.

One company that is doing a fantastic job in this regard is Walmart, which is responding to the market with their organic produce. The result is they have done pretty well in this down market. People shop there for low prices and the healthy food choices. In addition, Walmart is always innovating. In addition to the organic food, they have responded to their customers' needs with cheap prescription drugs and affordable family fun, with their new Family Night Centers.

Here is another example. Bill Palmer runs a service that repairs and sells high-speed drills to dentists in the Cincinnati market. Bill is very successful at what he does, having experienced tremendous growth and market penetration of over 60% of all dentists in the area. He understands a simple truth: Dentists use these tools of their trade every day. When a high-speed drill breaks, it hampers their business. So Bill completes his repairs in 24 hours and gets them back in the hands of the dentist faster than anyone else in the region. His customers value his speed and quality of service, and they keep coming back for more. His cost-of-sale numbers are low, and business is good.

Practice Exercise

To stay in the loop and know what your customers' needs are, call 10 of your top customers and ask them some leading questions.

Once you know the answers to these questions, you will have a good understanding of what is valuable to them today. These will be your fastest deals.

• How have their projects been reprioritized, given the economy?

_____

_____

_____

_____

_____

• What problems are being addressed in the next 6-12 months?

_____

_____

_____

_____

_____

- What problems are they committed to solving in the next 90 days?

_____

_____

_____

_____

_____

- How could you help them today?

_____

_____

_____

_____

_____

Part 4

THE PRINCIPLE OF PEOPLE

Step 16: KNOW YOUR CUSTOMERS

Step 17: MOVE POWERFULLY WITH TEAMS

Step 18: COMMUNICATE AND NETWORK

Step 19: FOLLOW THROUGH WITH EVERYONE

Step 20: ASK FOR REFERRALS

We are now ready to explore the fourth principle of **Wha-Dho**, the Principle of People. Many salespeople believe in the myth of the self-made success. According to this belief, the salesperson (or entrepreneur) succeeds because he or she possesses some innate genius or skill that virtually nobody else has. You have probably heard all about these people. You also have heard the stories told around the coffee pots and printed in the business magazines. In these stories, the hero conquers markets and makes fortunes. A lot of people fall in love with this dream; they become convinced that they too can be successful solely on their own. However, by the end of this part, you will have a more compelling strategy for success. You will learn how to enroll others in supporting you in accomplishing what you have set out to do.

- Who are the people in your circle of influence?
- Do they support you in your efforts to fulfill your vision?
- Do they sabotage your efforts to win?

Your overall success may very well depend on the answers to those three questions—especially when you must adapt to changing markets.

Every deal—every transaction and every business event—happens between people. You cannot survive without people, you cannot transact without people. you cannot reach your goals without people. The good news is that they need you too. Move in a way that allows you to align with people's needs that you can assist. If you are skilled at this analysis and assistance, you can help others reach their goals and improve their quality of life.

Let's review the last six months of your life.

- Were you involved in a sale that did not include other people?
- Was there a problem you solved that did not relate to people in some fashion?
- Did you do something and get paid by an entity with no people?

The answer to all three: of course not; there were always people involved, every step of the way. Each deal always revolves around people and their needs.

There's one clear way to leverage your skills and resources: Surround yourself with good, ethical people. The right people can be a powerful force-multiplier in your life. These are the people who can support you in fullfilling your goals and commitments; they will make all the difference to your success.

When I was working with the large-format printer in San Mateo, California, it was a new industry and new location (marketplace) for me. I frequently called on my friends for help and guidance. One of the people I reached out to was Sterling Lanier, the chair of one of the TEC groups (now called Vistage) in the area. When I needed referrals for recruiters or the best places to network to find new customers, I would call on Sterling. Within minutes, I had my answer or had access to the people who could help solve my business problems.

From the early days of our ancestors, back when we were cave dwellers, people had to coordinate and cooperate. It is in our DNA. My friend Rajesh Setty, a Silicon Valley entrepreneur and author, says it well: "It's all about the relationships." We were talking about a sale we had made with RawSugar, the Web-based content management and knowledge management application. We made the sale to the friend of a friend—an opportunity we would not have had if we had not leveraged the people in our lives.

Having powerful people in your life gives you the ability to work through the strategy and tactics you need to produce the results you are committed to achieving. It is also true that if you are committed to increasing revenue, especially in a tough or changing market, you are better off having friends in high places. They can help you open doors and introduce you to the right people.

The Market Has Changed Have You?

With this **Wha-Dho** Principle of People, you will learn to serve, support, nurture, leverage, and celebrate the people you have in your circle of influence.

The Principle of People

Step 16

KNOW YOUR CUSTOMERS

---

*The Market
Has Changed
Have You?*

Paul D'Souza

In Part Three, The Principle of Process, we talked about qualifying your prospects quickly. In that section, I mentioned the importance of building trust with your customers and prospects. Without trust, you will almost never close a deal. I believe the issue of trust deserves its own mention here, as we talk about the Principle of People. You cannot simply require your customers to extend trust to you; they must *choose* to trust you. You must earn their trust.

Know without a doubt that your customers need you to survive and do the things they cannot do by themselves. Have you ever looked at your customer relationships this way? If they did not need you, they would not talk to you. This could not be more true now, in these tough markets. They need help *now*.

- How well do you know your customers?
- Do you know them well enough to find out?

This is exactly what a sales call is all about. You must know your customers well enough to find out what they need help with. When you do, you will keep your sales activity grounded in something that your customer thinks is valuable. Once this happens, you will have higher close ratios. You will complete more transactions.

Know your customer profile as a demographic unit and as a group.

- Who are they?
- What problems do they have?
- What are their buying habits?
- How big is this market?

Know your customers as people:

- What are they like?
- What is important to them?
- What concerns do they have?
- What are they trying to accomplish?

Case in Point

When it comes to getting to know your customers as people, my friend Gerard Das is a master at the game. Through the years, I have noticed how he consistently gets in sync with his customers, building lasting friendships and relationships of trust. With these working relationships, you get access to their thinking, their trust and useful information about themselves, their companies and their industries. He is very professional in how he interacts with his customers, and reaps big rewards.

Gerard once caught a customer at her desk at 7:30 a.m. when he was expecting to leave a voice mail. He then learned she was an early riser, starting off at the gym at 5:00 a.m. A few weeks later he bought her a book about exercising, and it helped move their working relationship to a deeper level of trust.

In another conversation, Gerard heard that one of his customers was a military buff, so he got the customer a subscription to the military magazine he had been talking about. The customer was appreciative, and Gerard got an hour-long meeting that allowed him to gain a wealth of competitive information about the industry and a couple of good referrals.

Remember, it's all about the people you know.

Have integrity on how you go about interacting with them. Be of service and be nice to your customers. The relationships you develop are the space in which you will transact. So go built more working relationships of trust. You will close many more deals.

Practice Exercise

Know your customers well. Help them take care of themselves, their families, and their businesses. Build your customer relationships at a personal level and base them on truth, understanding, and integrity.

When you interact with your customers over the next two weeks, focus on these ideas:

- Listen to everything they are saying.
- Take notes and then take action.

Then do the following:

- Share information on a topic of interest.
- Buy them a book or something small.
- Help them with an introduction or referral.
- Take them out for lunch or coffee.

The more you know about the people you are dealing with, the more you will understand what is important to them; once you know what is important to them, you can respond to their needs. They will then begin to pay more attention to you. At this point, you might see the possibility of making an offer or a presentation. Remember, though, that you are still far from making a sale and closing the deal.

Ultimately, your offers will be accepted—i.e., your customers commit to giving you money—when you can solve their problems in a way they perceive as valuable and worth their investment.

The Principle of People

Step 17

MOVE POWERFULLY WITH TEAMS

*The Market
Has Changed
Have You?*

Paul D'Souza

In the United States, we greatly esteem corporate heroes who "go the distance," "never quit," "work alone," and are "confident risk takers." These kinds of heroes do well in television dramas, in the movies, and in our story books. But in the domain of business, these lone wolves are not very effective; they do not necessarily produce consistent results that you can bank on. In business and sales, it is the opposite of taking risks that helps you win in the long run. Risk costs money, heartache, and pain. If you're going to take advantage of opportunities in changing markets, you want to avoid the risks.

So, think about leverage. Think about how you can leverage all the people in your life to find opportunities and fulfill the promises that you make to your customers.

Let's look at a day in the life of a typical salesperson. As a sales associate or sales executive, you rely on a myriad of help from others to fulfill the promises you make to your customers. You need help producing the products and services you sell and you need help delivering them; later, you will also need help supporting your customers. The list goes on.

Here is a short list of the domains of activity that are needed to support the sale you made or are about to make.

- Marketing campaigns
- Product development
- Manufacturing and shipping infrastructure
- Computer systems and Web sites
- Support staff

I have not yet even started talking about the office support, finance, legal teams, and board of directors or investors of the company that make it all possible. You need these teams of people at one point or another to help you fulfill your promises.

When times become tough, you might be tempted to be a hero and work harder, smarter and go the distance alone. Instead, I invite you stop for a moment and thing about the people around you and try to indentify how you can build stronger relationships for the sake of winning more business.

Be attentive to everyone around you. Work respectfully with your peers and your customers. Think about your partners in creative ways, can you form effective working teams that compliment each other. Even if you close that big deal, you will most likely need a host of people to help you deliver and get paid.

Case in Point

Tushar Shah, who worked atVitria, sold a computer technology called Enterprise Application Integration—known as EAI in the industry. He was very good at what he did.

He brought in that "big fish"—a $15 million deal with Bell South, out of the Atlanta office, which did wonders for his career and his company. Bringing in a deal that big was no easy feat, of course, nor did he do it on his own. The sales cycle was long and he had help from the marketing staff, the inside sales team that made the initial contact, and his pre-sales engineers who helped demonstrate the software's ability. Then there were the legal teams that reviewed the contracts. The list goes on; you get the picture. The deal stuck, Tushar got paid, and went on to become a legend in the world of software sales. Without powerful teams supporting him on the deal, though, nothing would have happened.

In a changing marketplace, everyone seems stretched thin. In tough markets, we do not always have the luxury of spending time to learn things before we need to know them. We learn as we go. Emotions run high, dollars run low, and problems run amuck. Everybody needs good help, and so do you.

Since you need a lot of help just to survive, why not "up the ante" and make the support you get from others as powerful as possible? You will win tenfold for this investment in time and effort.

Practice Exercise

Build yourself a powerful team or a couple of different teams of people that you can work, coordinate, and collaborate with as you compete and move through the marketplace. You do not necessarily need to give yourselves a name and form an organization (legal entity) of any sort. But be clear about why you come together and how you can support each other. It's all about communication and a commitment to help each other fulfill your own objectives.

Your Career Team
Whom do you trust to help you develop your career?

_____

_____

Your Business Development Team
Whom can you coordinate and work with to maximize your business development efforts?

_____

_____

Your Personal Team
Who are the people in your life that nurture and support you?

_____

_____

Once you have these lists of people, reach out to them, reconnect with them, and enroll them in working with you. Get to deeper levels of connectedness and support. You can build these teams or networks of people to help you do a number of things. Consider working with a select group of people around specific projects or new-product initiatives. You might even create a group like this to work on a large sale or help open a new market segment to sell to.

Be open to the possibility of achieving more when you work with others to accomplish a common goal and support a common cause. I would also suggest you move with the times. Leverage the Internet and take the lead in connecting with people and communicate with your contacts on Web sites like FaceBook or LinkedIn, or even coordinate a meeting offline and start a group at Meetup.com.

The Market
Has Changed
Have You?

Paul D'Souza

Step 18

COMMUNICATE AND NETWORK

Deals are made between people—so, you must learn how to communicate and network effectively. Though everyone has limits when it comes to the amount of help they have access to, the more help you have, the more you can accomplish. Knowing how to communicate and network effectively will allow you to spend your time and resources in the most effective way. This is true in the marketplace as in life; it is not only what you know but who you know that really matters. Just as important is how well you know them. Good working relationships will help reduce your costs and increase your success when doing business.

The Market Has Changed Have You?

The Principle of People

Parker Thomson, a sales executive for one of the largest software companies in the world, takes a powerful approach when selling multimillion-dollar enterprise software deals. He once was working with McGraw-Hill, the publishing company, who was interested in doing business with a company called Tibco, one of his competitors. Parker used the power of networking and communicating to turn things around in his favor and win the deal. He calls his brand of networking "Networking with a Common Cause."

Parker worked with his implementation partner, Tata Consulting Services (TCS), to convince the people at McGraw-Hill that they would be better off in the long run if they went with his solution—even though it would bring TCS 25% less revenue. Now that's salesmanship!

How did Parker get McGraw-Hill to do that?

- He talked with every group at McGraw-Hill that had any influence on the project.
- He built rapport and good working relationships so that he could present his case on why his company's solution was better and cheaper.
- But he acknowledges the real convincing came from TCS.

Parker's "Networking with a Common Cause" provided a way for these organizations to work together for a common goal. It was a good way for TCS to strengthen their working relationships with one of the biggest software companies in the world. Improving that relationship was more valuable than the 25% revenue they would lose on this deal. Helping McGraw-Hill go with Parker's company was also the better business decision for the customer—which was the biggest reason they went this route.

Parker took the time to build relationships, communicate, and network with "everyone remotely connected to the deal," he noted. He showed McGraw-Hill the big picture and the benefits of working together in the long run. TCS played a big hand in showing McGraw-Hill how they would save even more money on upkeep and maintenance going with Parker's solution, helping to close the deal.

During the 2008 recession, companies scrambled to realign their expenses with declining revenues. They rushed to reduce their annual spending by tens of millions or even hundreds of millions of dollars. Imagine the budgetary pressure within these organizations. Every dime was scrutinized. CFOs routinely asked each department the same questions:

112

- How can we delay this expense?
- Can we reduce or eliminate this cost?
- What else can we do to save money?

Simply put, if you want to learn a prospect's needs, you must communicate and network with the right people at your target companies. Talk with them, build trust with them, and find out if there are certain things they need help with, things that you can do for them.Hanley Brite, founder of Authentic Connections, gave me this tip one day: When you call someone just to check in and see how they are doing, it's a networking call, and everybody loves it. But when you call someone and ask him or her to do you a favor, it sort of becomes a sales call. Learn to communicate and network; make more networking calls and fewer sales calls.

The Market Has Changed Have You?

The Principle of People

Practice Exercise

Increase the network of resources you are working with.

Take a moment to identify the "common causes" or "deals" around which you could potentially built powerful networks. Ground your networking activity around the projects you are working on, and link it directly to revenue. List the common causes you need to focus on in the next 90 days:

_____

_____

_____

_____

Now make lists of people you will need to reach out to. If you do not know the specific people, identify the titles, companies, or divisions you will need to access in the next 90 days to bring your deals to a close.

List of people you will reach out to:

_____

_____

_____

_____

_____

_____

_____

_____

Increase your circle of influence and your ability to transact with others. Doing this will help you interact with people you can do business with and who can help you fulfill your business goals and ambitions.

Step 19

FOLLOW THROUGH WITH EVERYONE

Following through with everyone you meet is a sure way to make certain that you do not miss any opportunities. In changing markets, you do not know where or when the next qualified opportunity will appear. Make sure you follow up on with everyone you talk to. You cannot afford to drop the ball and lose a deal. There are no shortcuts.

Susan Horner, who is mentioned in Step 8 in this book, sells a lot of real estate in Cincinnati. She says, "Every qualified offer is treated like gold," and then quickly adds, "Especially in today's market."

So whenever you think there might be a sliver of hope in someone making a deal with you, pay attention to it and work the opportunity. Qualify it accurately as soon as you can and then determine your next steps. If the lead qualifies, give it with more attention. If it does not qualify, move on quickly.

Let me also suggest that as a salesperson in a changing marketplace, you have to use your judgment and your time effectively. There are a higher percentage of deals that will not stick in a tough market. So when you notice a lead not qualifying, drop it fast, and move on to deals that have a better chance of coming to fruition.

Paul Staelin of www.birst.com, in an interview with Gerhard Gschwandtner of *Selling Power* magazine, says, "It is hard to make deals that are going slow, go faster. It's easier to focus your attention on the deals that are more likely to move fast. So analyze your deals by size, product, region, etc. Find out which deals are moving quickly. Are they installed base or not? Existing customers are already familiar with you and your product line. If you want your average sales cycle to go down...I would encourage you to, rather than doing the longer deals faster, focus on the faster deals."

I love this idea Paul Staelin proposes, because it is grounded in efficiency and a commitment to move powerfully through the market. Sales activity has two different types of tasks that need to work together:

1. Leverage your personal and interactive skills needed to engage and enlist your customers.
2. You need to follow strategic and systematic processes to be efficient with your time and resources.

It is a balance of art and science, and the good salespeople I know have learned to master this balance. You have to follow through with everyone you come across who could be a potential customer. In fact, I would also say that you even need to follow through with everyone who could help you get closer to a customer or help you influence and win a customer over.

Pick up the phone, meet people, have conversations, and follow through with all the connections you make. The surest way to be effective and not waste time while following up with all these people is to be clear about what you are trying to accomplish and then learn to ask good questions—questions that can help you qualify the people you need to transact with.

Practice Exercise

Make lists of prospects you have met in the past two years. Call on them, reestablish your rapport with them, and ask an important question. Find out what their strategic initiatives are for the next 12 months. Find out what help they need now and, if appropriate, ask them for their business.

I suggest that you start by making a list of 50 people whom you can call over the next few days. Put your contacts in groups and reconnect and follow through on the most logical choices given the economy and what you have set out to do.

- Start with a phone call.
- Based on what you hear, you can choose your next steps like e-mail, newsletters, and other ways to follow through.

Contact	Phone	Problem	Next Steps

Resources

To learn more about understanding human behavior, establishing powerful relationships and enhancing rapport with your customers, consider reviewing the work of Tom Vizzini and Kim McFarland at www.essential-skills.com.

Step 20

ASK FOR REFERRALS

---

*The Market
Has Changed
Have You?*

Paul D'Souza

If you are an experienced salesperson, then you know the power of referrals (warm leads). They make life so much easier, and they accelerate the velocity of your sales cycles. With referrals, you can turn a potential cold call into a warm conversation. You can establish rapport faster; you can learn your prospect's problems faster; and you can work your way to a deal faster. All you have to do is ask for that referral—and ask for one whenever you can and as often as you can.

Very often I find sales associates walking away from a customer or a sales opportunity without asking for a referral. Don't do that! Learn when to ask for referrals and make sure you learn the correct way to do it. Not asking for a referral is a mistake that is like leaving money on the table, and could mean losing opportunities to make a sale—opportunities that are very scarce in tough and changing markets. You spent valuable time building a relationship with a prospect, walking away from that prospect without asking for a referral is just too costly. Being able to get referrals will save you time and money, but remember that you still have to work these opportunities like any other.

Asking for referrals is an art form. It takes some practice to do it well. Timing is critical. Avoid asking for a referral too early or too often. Yet, it is important, especially in tough markets, to leverage the relationships you have in the market and ask your customers to refer you to people who could use your services. I take this process seriously. I believe without a shadow of a doubt that what I have to offer people is valuable and important. I genuinely want to meet them and help if possible. You should too.

Very often, we come across several opportunities when we can ask for a referral—and there are several ways to ask. I strongly believe that salespeople can ask for referrals even before they have consummated the sale. In talking with my peers, I find that many of us do this successfully and often. I would highly recommend you consider doing the same, especially in today's difficult marketplace.

A few years ago, I sold IT services to the medical communications departments of large pharmaceutical companies throughout the United States. One might think that the pharmaceutical industry is huge, and it is, but the medical communications folks are a smaller, tight-knit group of people in close touch with each other. Since the sales cycles on these deals were very long, I got into the practice of successfully asking for referrals as soon as I developed a good rapport with my prospects.

This worked very well, and soon I was being introduced to medical communication specialists and directors at pharmaceutical companies all over the country, resulting in selling about $9 million worth of IT services over a three-year period.

I believe there are two things needed before you can ask for referrals. They are;

- A good rapport with your customer.
- A reputation of trust and value.

You should never ask for a referral without meeting both of those requirements. If you lack either one, your prospects and customers will hesitate to introduce you to their friends and peers.

If you try to push a referral anyway, you will most probably damage whatever working relationship you have, and could even jeopardize the deal you are working on.

However, once you meet both requirements, you should always ask for referrals. Your silence would waste a good lead-generation opportunity.

Ask yourself the following questions:

- How much does my contact trust me?
- Why would someone refer me to one of his or her friends?
- What request would be appropriate?
- Should I ask my contact to give me a name, make the call, or send out an introduction via e-mail?

Just as a trial lawyer asks only the question he or she already knows the answer to, you should know what your contact would do for you before asking for a referral.

I do not believe there are any shortcuts here. You must have trust with your contact and something valuable to offer their friends before an introduction will be made. Once you meet both requirements, though, go for it.

Practice Exercise

Asking for referrals is like making a sale. In effect, it requires you to close a deal, but in this case, the sale you make is a sale of trust. Get comfortable asking seemingly tough questions. Learn to stay in control of your conversations, work to build rapport fast but without crowding the prospect, and always sell something of value. In the next three days, I would like you to call on 10 people you have good working relationships with (relationships of trust). Ask them to introduce you to a potential customer, and have them explain to you why they think the referral will be a good fit.

Here are three steps to guide these calls:

Introduce
Yourself and check in with them.

Inquire
About something of importance to them.

Request
A referral—be clear and specific.

Make these calls. Be relaxed when you are speaking with your contact, and remember to breathe. I am not kidding! Take a few breaths and have a friendly conversation with them. Your customers should be your friends.

Leverage the relationship of trust you have with them, and ask them for a referral. I promise—you will be amazed at how you will increase the number of opportunities you have to work on. You will also be able to accelerate deals you are currently pursuing, because you will be engaged in better conversations with people.

List three contacts you can call on today or tomorrow and ask for a referral.

Contact 1 _____

Referrals _____

_____

_____

Contact 2 _____

Referrals _____

_____

_____

Contact 3 _____

Referrals _____

_____

_____

122

*The Market
Has Changed
Have You?*

The Principle
of People

*The Market
Has Changed
Have You?*

Paul D'Souza

Part 5

THE PRINCIPLE OF PRACTICAL LEADERSHIP

Step 21: BE THE EXPERT

Step 22: BE NIMBLE

Step 23: EMPOWER OTHERS TO WIN

Step 24: BE PROACTIVE WITH YOUR CUSTOMERS

Step 25: SAY THANK YOU ALWAYS

124

Let us now turn our attention to the fifth and final principle of the **Wha-Dho** sales strategy, the Principle of Practical Leadership. To leverage this thinking effectively, I suggest you follow the guidelines in this book and work through the first four principles. Doing so will give you the ability to leverage this fifth principle to a very high degree. In my experience, the rewards are usually disproportionately related to effort: Small efforts yield big returns. You may say, "I'm a salesperson, not a leader, so how will I use the Principle of Practical Leadership?" Here is how to do it. I used to sell business intelligence and data warehousing software to the enterprise market. I recently spoke with a friend who is now a sales engineer with the Cognos software company, which is a sales support role. He asked me how someone like him could leverage the Principle of People and the Principle of Practical Leadership in his life. Here's the basics of what I told him:

1. Start by being clear about your vision and what you want to accomplish in life.
2. Know how much money you need for your vision.
3. Understand how your current job as a sales engineer supports that vision.
4. Enroll people in your circle of influence to support your strategy to fulfill your vision.
5. Move with Practical Leadership to enhance your cause and fulfill your vision.

I embedded the **Wha-Dho** sales strategy into every step of this outline which he could follow tomorrow and begin working toward his vision of success.

Adopting a leader's mental perspective and a maintaining a leadership mood will help you increase your sense of practical leadership. You will begin to care for the people you lead and begin to nurture their fulfillment of their own dreams and goals. That is what leaders do. They lead people to a better tomorrow.

The ripple effect of that caring and nurturing is a powerful spur to accomplish whatever goal you are committed to achieving, because you will begin to reap the benefits of loyalty, support, and commitment from your colleagues, your customers, and your partners. You gave first in leading them to a brighter future and the possibility of power and prosperity, and now they are ready to reciprocate. This is the human experience at its most rewarding. Leverage this core behavior in your sales and business activity.

Do these outcomes make you want to become a leader? They should encourage you to think of the possibility. Fix these two questions in your mind:

- Do I think and act like a leader?
- Do I support the people around me to act as leaders?

Imagine the levels of efficiency and effectiveness that are possible when everyone on your team holds these principles and works toward their collective goals. Magical things will happen!

When I worked with a company in Georgia that manufactured spectrophotometers, we used these principles; I found that the employees began holding the Principle of Practical Leadership early in my relationship with them. In their own sphere of responsibility they started to think as leaders, which touched how they looked at their jobs and their role in the organization. They started thinking proactively and helped change how we did business, making suggestions that would help in several ways.

This attitude changed everything. Problems were solved before they escalated. We were selling to people who had not bought from us before. Existing customers were buying more. Our production time dropped, helping increase cash flow. We were collectively being creative and innovative. We went from a place where morale was low to a place where employees enjoyed working and wanted their relatives and friends to work with us as well.

One notable example was related to customer service. The employees suggested a new approach to handling incoming customer calls; that was much better than what we were doing all along. When we implemented this new approach, the number of calls that escalated to where a manager had to get involved dropped sharply. The additional benefit was that we started using the customer service experience with customers to build better relationships, giving us more opportunities to sell them additional services and upgrades. The sales team and customer service staff started working together to serve their customers better. Things started to change and revenues grew about 60% in 18 months. We made many changes, but each employee, individually, started thinking and acting like a leader—proactively producing results that supported corporate goals.

The results were truly remarkable, showing that practical leadership will help you and your organization achieve higher levels of productivity and profit. When you think and act like a leader, you provide the impetus for the five principles of the **Wha-Dho** sales strategy to work together.

Let's briefly review what you have learned in the first four principles of the philosophy:

1. You are clear about your vision and sense of purpose.
2. You know how much money your vision requires.
3. You designed starategies and tactics to make the money to fulfill your vision.
4. You have leveraged the people in your circle of influence to accomplish more.

Now it's time to empower yourself and your teams with practical leadership so they produce more, have better work experiences, accelerate everyone's success, and achieve victory.

Step 21

BE THE EXPERT

Everyone loves an expert. Being the expert is one of the fastest ways to build trust with your customers. You will be able to open doors because of who you are.

The Market Has Changed Have You?

The Principle of Practical Leadership

Think about the situation from your customer's perspective. A changing marketplace isn't the time for you to be saying "I don't know." If your prospects are desperately trying to adapt to a changing environment, expect them to be prudent and cautious about doing business with you or anybody else. They will not spend money on anything risky or when they have any doubt about the effectiveness of a solution they are trying to implement. A poor purchasing decision may cause them to lose their job or stunt their career.

In changing marketplaces, even though they might not risk, people look for help and advice. They want experts to solve problems for them and help them get through these tough markets. So be the expert. Be the help they're searching for!

Don't forget that most customers are usually looking for help, either with advice or hands-on problem solving. When you are the expert, customers will gravitate to you, give you their trust, and want to transact with you. The more you can prove you know what you are talking about and have the ability to take care of them, the more they will trust you enough to transact with you.

There is a lot of buzz in the marketplace today about education-based marketing. Chet Holmes, in his book *The Ultimate Sales Machine*, talks about how you should act strategically and not tactically. He focuses on the value in leveraging educational programs that demonstrate your thought leadership and expertise in your given field of work.

There is tremendous value in educating your customers; it conveys your value and helps you build trust with your customers. During these educational programs (make sure they are not sales calls or sales presentations), prospects genuinely feel educated on the subject you are talking about. The more you take the lead in providing them honest, legitimate information that can help them understand their problems, the more informed they will be to make a decision that is good for them. And if you are smart about how you go about this process, this also will work out tremendously well for you and your company.

Cognos, the data warehousing and business intelligence software company, would on a quarterly basis organize two-hour learning sessions. Cognos would bring in a recognized expert in some aspect of data warehousing and have him or her give customers and prospects a learning session on the subject. These were fantastic opportunities where, with a little effort, the right prospects would be enrolled to think about the problems they were dealing with in an environment created for them. Learning sessions like these consistently helped advance the nature of the relationship Cognos had with their prospects. For the companies that attended these breakfast learning sessions, Cognos very quickly became the preferred go-to organization for help related to data warehousing and business intelligence.

The Story of Chateaux Software

I recently had a conversation with Mark Montanaro, a principal at Chateaux Software, a 25-year-old business intelligence consulting firm.

Chateaux had managed to grow its business without a dedicated marketing manager, but since the market changed, so did they! Here are some things they began doing:

- Chateaux has started to talk about and further expose its expertise. With over 25 highly specialized consultants solving customer problems daily for 25 years, you know the company has some good stories to tell—but it was not leveraging them. It is now, and it is working very well for the company.

- Chateaux started a newsletter a couple of years ago and built the distribution to about 30,000 people, pretty extensive for such a niche market. The company has also increased the quality of the content in these distributions to make the newsletter consistently informative and useful.

- Chateaux has started doing very focused learning events. It takes a subject, let's say Data Quality for the Enterprise market, which is focused to start with, but then takes it a couple of steps deeper and talks about "Real-Time Data Quality for E-Commerce," a small part of overall Data Quality in the Enterprise market. What Chateaux has found is that these highly focused workshops produce results. They recently got a call from a Fortune 100 company the day after one of their its workshops; asking Chateaux to come in and help with exactly what they talked about. Being the expert (and demonstrating it) paid off!

Practice Exercise

Identify three topics of interest and host three learning events in the next six months. Make sure your topics of education are current and of significant value to your customers. I would suggest you go deeper and narrower, focusing on niche markets and smaller groups of qualified prospects, instead of trying to attract broad categories of interest that tend to bring in large numbers of unqualified prospects.

Once you select topics, test them with some of your key customers. Make sure that your topics interest enough to attend.

Event One

Date: _____ *(in the next 2 months)*

Topic: _____

Solution it supports: _____

Event Two

Date: _____ *(4 months from now)*

Topic: _____

Solution it supports: _____

132

Event Three

Date: _____ *(6 months from today)*

Topic: _____

Solution it supports: _____

Begin this thinking process now, before you move on to the end of this book. Put your initial thoughts down in the spaces above. You will be amazed at how "not difficult" this is once you get going. You can always find the thought leaders and experts later.

Make the effort, push yourself, do more, and become "the expert" in your chosen field of work: no exceptions and no excuses. Increase your ability, your skills, and your resources to solve real problems for your customers; they will thank you and reward you for the value you bring them.

Step 22

BE NIMBLE

When you join management experts and embrace the idea of practical leadership, you will realize that occasions will arise when you will have to react quickly and powerfully to regain control of a situation during a sales process, especially in changing markets. Be attentive to what your customers are doing and saying. When you observe the beginning stages of a trend, pay attention and move quickly. It's about solving your customers' problems, not yours, so work with customers, move with them, and provide them with the solutions they need. In a changing market, customers often have urgent needs that they might not know how to solve themselves. If you have a reputation of being an expert, they will want you to help them design a solution that works for them. Be the expert, react quickly, and take charge—but always communicate with your customers and ensure that they feel they still have control over how things are going on "their" project. Sound paradoxical? It is—but it works.

Be proactive in your customers' lives; it is not enough to be order takers only. Our sales guys have to really work an account, fighting our way in. In changing markets, the complexity of deals and the probability of deals going south is exceedingly high. Every market segment will be different, but be prepared for a different set of rules now. You must stay alert to your customers' needs and learn to respond to them fast.

As an example, here is how I converted a $30,000 software deal into a $740,000 consulting engagement. I was working with RWD Technologies as their partner liaison. This entailed helping them manage their relationships with larger software companies like Documentum and Siebel. We had built a piece of software that connected these two applications and my job was to work with the sales team at Documentum, helping them sell this new product we built.

When qualifying the prospect's interest in the software, I just happened to ask him how his company was going to implement something that no one else but us on the entire planet knew anything about. This was asking the tough business questions. What then transpired was a very intense sales situation where we had to oust the incumbent vendors that had a good working relationship with the prospect. We demonstrated our capabilities and won the deal. The rest, as they say, is history. We went on to have a lot of success over the next 3 years.

In changing markets, you will come across situations that require you to be flexible, creative, and powerful in how you respond. Here are some examples:

- You might have to get creative on how you do financing.
- Your customers might have a new approval process.
- Customers may be looking for reduced costs in service delivery.
- Government regulations might have changed, changing customers' needs.
- Technology changes have altered the way customers do business.
- You industry itself might vanish.

Take whatever information your customers are giving you and make powerful assessments about how you might be able to assist them. Here is another example. Susan Horner, the real estate agent in Cincinnati, is constantly flexible and attuned to her customers' needs as she talks with them. I remember how when working with me and my wife she would constantly take the lead in reconfiguring her search criteria based on what she heard in our conversations. As we saw homes, our criteria changed. Sounds familiar in your world, with your customers? Susan was nimble, and helped us find our desired home. within two weeks from Hello to Close.

Practice Exercise

If you want to become nimble, you must learn from your misses. Reflect on the last few deals you lost. Ask yourself these questions:

What were the specific problems or conditions your prospects had that you could not solve?

_____

_____

_____

_____

How might I solve them today, if I had that opportunity again?

_____

_____

_____

_____

Am I noticing other/similar trends now?

_____

_____

_____

_____

Review your notes. Revisit your deals. See if you would do anything differently.

- Did you miss an opportunity to act powerfully?
- Did you demonstrate your thought leadership?
- Did you miss cues your customers gave you?

Step 23

EMPOWER OTHERS TO WIN

Most salespeople focus on the deals that will close quickly and help make their numbers and commissions. I would call this the short-term strategy. It is a valid strategy and it must be done, but there is more.

When you build your career strategically, you will realize how important it is to surround yourself with powerful people who can help you fulfill on your commitments. One of the most effective ways to do this is to empower others to win. Support people around you to accomplish their goals and they will bend over backward to take care of you and help you along the way.

I once had a customer named Ken Frost, who worked for Immunex, a small biotech out of Seattle, that was later bought by Amgen. Ken and I became good friends during the course of the project, and I remember asking him on several occasions what was important to him as an individual and the company at large. I learned that it was important for their team to implement this project and make sure it went off without a hitch. Completing the project in budget was good, and bringing it in less than budget would have been fantastic. I also learned that Ken was in sort of a tight spot. The users of this new application wanted their old system back, but, he had to ensure they used this new program; on the other hand, he had to protect his own career and satisfy his ultimate boss, the CIO. In short, it had to be a successful project with everone satisfied.

As salespeople, we have to help our customers win and succeed and do well in their jobs at the companies they work for. I remember being particularly sensitive with Ken's user community because they had voiced concerns to him, so I flew in extra consultants to work with them and help them through the user acceptance testing process. We also needed to show certain deliverables before a specific date for various internal requirements important to Ken and his team, so we designed the project in phases to meet these requirements. Throughout the project, we were very sensitive to Ken's needs, which helped our working relationship and took our project through completion of the second phase with a total billing of over $1,200,000.

It need not take much effort to make a difference in other people's lives. I do think that small, thoughtful acts of kindness, consideration, and generosity can be applied in almost any situation. Take care of people around you; ask them a simple yet incredibly powerful question: "How can I help?" Go out of your way to help people that you meet. Remember that every call, every deal, every transaction is done between people. Be attentive to all the people in your active world—from the receptionist and other gatekeepers you encounter, to the mid-level managers, and all the way up to the C-level executives you meet.

Let me give you another story. I was talking to John, a friend who worked for the State of New York. He told me how Honeywell once flew him to their very impressive facilities someplace in Texas. They flew him in their private jet, wined and dined him and his colleagues for a couple of days, and flew him back. Unfortunately, according to him, the strategy did not work, because they forgot to ask him what his needs were. Their competitor, IBM, took the time to focus on John's business requirements. He was not flown to

The Market
Has Changed
Have You?

The Principle
of Practical
Leadership

their facilities nor was he entertained, but they did provide a service he needed. They took care of him. All he wanted was to do his job better. IBM met that objective, so he naturally rewarded them with his business and did not switch vendors, despite the lavish trip and informative tours Honeywell gave him.

When you empower others to win, they will want to keep you close. They will want to support you, and they will want to return the favor. But there is also a deeper level of trust being built. They know you will take care of them when they need help sometime in the future. You start becoming a partner in their business and in their life; in essence, you stop selling and you start "working together." Your cost-of-sale comes down and profits go up.

In Japan, they take this concept of reciprocity to very deep levels of trust and partnership. Once a company chooses a vendor, they work on developing a relationship of trust with each other. They support each other as people and as business partners. Switching vendors is very rare. If done, it is done very carefully and with a lot of consideration, because it could be a costly endeavor with tremendous risk.

Howard Stevens of HR Chally and the University Sales Education Foundation (USEF) recently spoke about how the Japanese and other East Asian business societies, focus their sales initiatives on keeping customers and growing existing accounts. They do go after new customers, but they focus more attention on their existing customers, helping them get more out of their relationship. Help your customers do more with their involvement with you. It's a fantastic way to grow your business.

140

Practice Exercise

It's really about developing the ability to connect with people and being sensitive to their needs. Notice, observe, and ask questions that get them connecting with you and sharing with you what is important to them. This is practical leadership. This is practical leadership at its best.

The Market Has Changed Have You?

The Principle of Practical Leadership

Make a list of your top five contacts. Call them in the next week, and ask them how you can help them with something of importance. Ask them specifically about their employee reviews (if this is appropriate) and find out how you might be able to help them get a good one. If this does not apply, ask them something like this:

- What are your strategic initiatives for the rest of the year?
- Which projects are you committed to completing now?
- Do you foree problems with any of them?
- What keeps you up at night these days?

Contact 1: _____

Opportunity: _____

Contact 2: _____

Opportunity: _____

Contact 3: _____

Opportunity: _____

Contact 4: _____

Opportunity: _____

Contact 5: _____

Opportunity: _____

Empower people to win, and they will want to do more with you. You will be amazed at how this will change the quality of your interactions. I invite you to share your stories with me.

Step 24

BE PROACTIVE WITH YOUR CUSTOMERS

Making a sale is always about solving problems; remind yourself about this always. I will never forget what Gerhard Gschwandtner, the founder and CEO of *Selling Power* magazine, once said to me: "Give me something I can take to my customers that can help them sell more, and then get out of my way! That will be a lot of fun."

Gerhard believes in being proactive in the customer's world. He lives this idea of bringing new, exciting, useful, and valuable products and services to sales professionals across the globe, and he does this better than anyone I know. All of us in the world of sales owe him a big debt of gratitude for helping the field mature in stature and professionalism.

As a sales professional who is committed to increasing revenue and profits for your organization, consider taking a personal stand. Get to know your customers well, build trust, and engage with them. Then, become a proactive and a protective force they can come to rely upon. Take your customers' interests to heart and watch your life change.

In this marketplace, most companies are doing their best to survive and do more with less. Your customers need all kinds of help. How can you make a difference? Use this situation as an opportunity to do some thinking on behalf of your customers and go that extra mile—get out there and do something different that will shock the heck out of your prospects and customers. Be proactive; take the lead and the initiative to engage. This is not the time to wait for customers to call you and place an order. Get up and get moving!

When you are grounded in helping your customers, you will do more in the marketplace. The better and more consistently you can do this, the more your customers will want to transact with you. Apple does it fantastically well. They have that One-on-One program, where $99 gets you 52 one-on-one sessions with an expert—in essence, one session a week. During this session, they help you with any questions you might have in using your computer; they will work with you at your level and help you do more with your investments in their products. I have used these sessions extensively and have loved them. The better I got at using their products, the more Apple products I bought! Makes perfect sense, doesn't it?

It's not about just completing a one-time deal or a single transaction. You genuinely take your customers' concerns to heart and, with sincerity and integrity, bring them solutions and services they need to take care of their problems. The difference is that you are partnering with them in your collective future.

There are many businesses where a one-time transaction may be the norm. Chances are, though, that those people are not reading this book, which is focused on the long term and on lasting working relationships with their customers—definitely the more profitable approach to take. It also reduces your cost-of-sale and increases your profit margins. I am suggesting that you be proactive in your customers' lives because it is the fastest way to get closer to your sales numbers, and it helps you increase your profits.

For me, the beautiful thing about sales is that the more you can find ways to help your customers, the more you will be rewarded for it.

144

Sales is the process of helping people make good decisions that will take care of problems or promote interests they might have. Most often, making a sale improves the quality of someone's life. Be that proactive force that takes care of people.

Practice Exercise

Pick your top 10 customers and get to know them well. Do the following in the next two weeks: Have conversations with them over the phone, via e-mail, at lunch, or with coffee—whatever feels appropriate. People do business with people they trust and like.

1. Map out their universe and understand what is important to them. What business sectors do they watch? What trends are they looking for?
2. Learn the top 10 concepts that drive their business; this will help you get in sync. More important, you will become an insider.
3. Network with complementary organizations in their industry to gain industry knowledge and new relationships, increasing your ability to solve their problems.

Sample table to help you gather information

Customer	Business Interests	Key Concepts	Networking
Internet technology company	Technology trends, social media, Internet revenue models, angel and venture funding, skilled labor	Technology, funding, interactive marketing, content management, GUI design	ACG, Silicon Valley Bank, Joint Venture, SVASE, SVMN, Band of Angels, Kleiner Perkins
Bob Henry			
Rebecca James			
Pharmaceutical company	FDA and any new guidelines, clinical trials news, Wall Street news, global demographic trends, CDC reports	Medical data reporting, adverse-effects reporting guidelines, FDA guidelines —Phase 4 clinical trials, package insert regulations	DIA, PDE, Ph RMA, DCAT, Institute for Safe Medical Practices

146

Step 25

SAY THANK YOU ALWAYS

You don't miss thanking your friends for things they do, including the things they do in very personal and often creative ways. Why do you treat your customers differently? I have never liked those corporate cards that say thank you for your order. So what if you wrote the address by hand; it is still a copout. Go the extra mile, and get beyond that level of pretense. Be human; find out what your customer likes, and get him or her a real gift. How about a book or a membership to a favorite magazine, or a shaving kit for business travel, or even tickets to a ball game or other sports event?

The Market Has Changed Have You?

The Principle of Practical Leadership

I, for one, was very successful with Starbucks gift cards. And when you lose a deal, which can happen for a million different reasons, how about reaching back out to the person you worked with and close the loop with a "thank you for your time and your interest in what we do" gift. This is what a true sales leader would do. That person will appreciate it, and could very well end up being a fantastic resource for leads and referrals.

Gratitude is one of the most powerful emotions you can use to strengthen your bonds with other people. This goes back to the fundamentals of human behavior. There is something visceral that happens when we say thank you. Immediately, we move from stranger to friend and from being a potential threat to being a positive resource in each other's life. Saying thank you is also anchored in the belief that we are, at our core, beings of love, and that we like being appreciated at every opportunity.

Saying thank you in a powerful way is just that—powerful. Learn to do it. In the business of sales, we are dead without our working relationships. Be genuinely interested in the people who make up your professional universe. Appreciating what people do for you and saying thank you will help you build robust relationships that you can bank on. I suggest you make a standard practice and find ways to say thank you to your customers and prospects as often as possible.

Irina Haydon, Executive Director of Sales at Heartland Payment Systems, expresses it well. She talks about our needing to be grateful to our customers for giving us the opportunity to engage in sales activity with them; becoming partners in their business comes later, after trust is established. She goes on to explain how customers have the ability to sense your true intentions. They have a million things going on in their lives and when you come along and ask them for 10-15 minutes to look at your offer, you are in effect taking something very precious away from them—their time! Take your customers seriously and be prepared; what you say must have significant value to them.

Irina suggests that you embrace a deeper sense of gratitude and sensitivity in how you approach your customers and let this sense be reflected in how you think and act with them. They will feel your emotional maturity, sensitivity, and appreciation. In time, you will notice how you have become intuitive about their actions and be one step ahead of them when overcoming obstacles. As a sales leader, Irina is constantly coaching her sales associates to imagine that they are bringing a wrapped gift when seeing a customer. The question is, What is in the box? How did you wrap it? Did you think how the customer would react? These gifts may come in the guise of providing prospects with valuable knowledge of new

148

information they can use despite the outcome of their meetings. This is "gratitude in action," going way beyond the spoken words of thank you. This is about giving something without expecting anything in return. And it works. In 1999 Heartland Payment Systems was the 56th largest company in transactions volume; today, its the 4th largest company in their space.

This is a conversation about conveying your gratitude and thanks. Say thank you often, and get good at saying it sincerely and powerfully. Always proceed with a heart true to your career and your customers' interests.

The Market Has Changed Have You?

The Principle of Practical Leadership

While I was at RWD Technologies, I had a customer, Karla Manns Giroux, who worked at a large pharmaceutical firm in Chicago. She was the lead person on a project team that was interested in our technology solution. Unfortunately for both of us, the firm could not commit to taking action on a project for about 18 months for various internal reasons. All through this process, we worked together, moving the deal along, and I would thank her for the effort she took in coordinating with her team and their corporate processes. Our working relationship deepened to levels of mutual trust and understanding to the point that, before they closed on a deal with us, Karla was helping me with industry-specific information and introductions to her peers at other pharmaceutical companies, which helped us at RWD Technologies win more business.

This human characteristic of being grateful for the help we receive is a force that moves our society. It has been like this for eons, and it is something we should all be using in business to enhance our cause and compete powerfully in the marketplace. Gratitude and cooperation, in my opinion, are the very forces that move business along, dropping costs and increasing profits. Did you know that in

Japan there is a business practice of giving gifts to customers and partners, not only at the end of the year, as we do here in the United States, but also in summer? The Japanese are very appreciative of their customers and business partners, and they celebrate it. Once a customer has chosen a vendor, they pretty much stay committed; the vendor thus sells once and services the account over and over again. It is also a very profitable way of doing things.

Practice Exercise

The 7in7 Campaign

As salespeople, we are always caught in the middle. On one side, we have our external customers and prospects that we have to work with to find opportunities, qualify them, make presentations to, and win business. And on the other, we have our internal customers, all the people we work with within our organizations who help in the sales process and later in delivering the solution or the product we sell. They all count. Over the next seven days, say thank you to seven people who contribute to your success. Do something personal and different in your thank you; no cookie-cutter corporate cards allowed.

- Say thank you to the gatekeepers you work with.
- Say thank you to prospects for considering your offer.
- Say thank you to customers for their business.
- Say thank you to your colleagues who help you close deals.

Reach out to everyone who has contributed to your deals, because they could make or break your chances to succeed.

Final Thoughts and the 90-Day Plan

The market has changed, and now you have! You not only read this book, but you completed the practice exercises and made changes to your life as a person and as a sales professional. You now are poised to operate with a clear sense of purpose and act powerfully in the marketplace. Your actions will be deeply rooted in the principles of the **Wha-Dho** philosophy. With a winning attitude and a powerful strategy, you will be able to take advantage of the opportunities you see. You will achieve success in this or any other market.

Markets change all the time. They go through cycles of inflation, and then they go through cycles of deflation. These changes happened before, and they will happen again. Now, you can ride these waves of change and be prepared either way they go.

When others bellyache or lament change, you will be motivated to detect new sales opportunities and redefine your offer to the marketplace. You will as well always operate in alignment with your personal goals.

In tough times, we need to be as powerful as we can possibly be. Tap into the deeper resources of yourself and access your true power, your creative genius, and your passion.

Some of the best business stories revolve around someone who had a seemingly crazy vision. That person applied personal strength and turned that vision into reality. That's how you leapfrog over the competition—both in tough changing markets as well as in booming growth markets. You always position yourself to thrive and win.

Now, let us take a look at the final step. So far, you have applied individual principles of the **Wha-Dho** sales strategy in bits and pieces through your journey of reading this book. I now suggest that you take on a more rigorous 90-day program that uses this philosophy to make serious change in your life. This program will allow you to work through these five principles to produce specific outcomes you choose to commit to accomplishing in the next 90 days.

The 90-Day Plan

Use the practices and exercises in this book over the next 90 days and create a future that is powerful, useful, and worth your investments of time, energy, and money. Start by taking stock of where you are now. With those findings you will be able to design a powerful strategy to produce a valuable outcome that will improve the quality of your life.

The Market Has Changed Have You?

The Principle of Practical Leadership

- Let us review where you are now.
- Which of the exercises in the book produced the most powerful results for you?
- How can you replicate this success?

_____

_____

_____

- What did you learn from reaching back to your customers while reading this book?
- How was this different from what you did in the past?

_____

_____

_____

- Have you changed your offer to the marketplace? If so, does it reflect the current needs of your customers?
- Do you need to change it further?

- Are you clearer about your sense of purpose?
- Are you excited about what you want to accomplish in life?
- Do you need to work on this further?

Step One—Purpose and Vision: Week 1

- Do you need to work on your vision at this time?
- Are you clear about what you are trying to accomplish in life?

Step Two—Money and Prosperity: Week 1

- How much money are you going to make in 90 days?
- Do you have any other financial conditions to satisfy?

_____

_____

_____

_____

The Market Has Changed Have You?

5

The Principle of Practical Leadership

Step Three—Process Definition: Week 1–Week 3

- Design a powerful strategy for fulfilling your vision.
- Begin executing on the structure and organization of your process.

_____

_____

_____

_____

Step Four—Assessment of People: Week 2 onward

- Who are the people you will be working with? Who else will help you accomplish your goals?
- Have you secured their commitment? If not, what do you need to enroll them into your vision?

_____

_____

_____

_____

Step Five—Assessment of Leadership: Week 4 onward

- Are you thinking like a leader and taking charge of your project?
- Are you empowering the others you are working with to think and act like leaders?

_____

_____

_____

_____

Step Six—Recap & Redesign: Day 91

- Did you accomplish your goals?
- What can you leverage moving forward?
- Begin Designing your next projects.

_____

_____

_____

_____

The Market Has Changed Have You?

The Principle of Practical Leadership

Coaching on the 90-Day Plan

Once you are clear about your vision and commitment, you will be able to make powerful assessments of value, helping you be more effective in what you do. Every person you meet, situation you have, and action you take will either support or sabotage your efforts to fulfill your vision.

When picking something to work on, be very clear about the consequences you will face if you do NOT fulfill your criteria for success. This will create the appropriate sense of urgency and call to action that you will need to be successful.

When designing what you do, seek to be efficient and effective. Build in checkpoints that assess your development. Watch for benchmarks of success along the way. Be ready to change your tactics if they are not producing the results you seek.

Leverage people in your circle of influence. Take the time to know what is important to them before you ask them to help you. Learn to enroll them into working with you and to coordinate with them in a way that helps them meet their own goals.

Empower others to win every step of the way. This will create a space for you to leverage everything you do.

The market has changed—have you? It's time!

Space for additional thinking about your future.

*The Market
Has Changed
Have You?*

The Principle
of Practical
Leadership

Long-Term Strategic Plan

Now that you have a good understanding of the **Wha-Dho** Sales Strategy; leverage this thinking and design a powerful strategy to build yourself a better future. Increase your horizons of time to work in 18-month segments. Use the 5 Principles of Change and the 25 Steps as background thinking to help you be effective in the market place.

Phase 1	Develop a Strong Platform
Time Line	January 2010 thru June 2011
Capital at Work	$ 100,000 (be realistic)
Annual Income	$ 80,000 (be realistic)
Approach	How will you go about doing this? Specify a Job or Business Project 1. Specify a Job or Business Project 2.

Phase 2	Leverage your Market Value
Time Line	July 2011 thru December 2012
Capital at Work	$
Annual Income	$
Approach	Leverage your relationships and experience. Design a more powerful offer. Start a new business maybe.

Phase 3	Build Assets and Investments
Time Line	January 2013 thru June 2014
Capital at Work	$
Annual Income	$
Approach	Invest in Real Estate of other Businesses. Start another company yourself. Expand your current business.

Phase 4	Leverage Assets and Lifestyle
Time Line	July 2014 thru December 2015
Capital at Work	$
Annual Income	$
Approach	You are living a powerful life. You have created an effective empire. Your business activity is making money.

*The Market
Has Changed
Have You?*

The Principle
of Practical
Leadership

About the Author

The Market
Has Changed
Have You?

Paul D'Souza

Paul D'Souza is a revenue generator and a sales professional who enjoys helping people solve problems while motivating them into better ways of doing things. He has worked in several industries and has held various types of sales positions—from knocking on doors selling frozen meats to holding several VP of sales roles and helping bring in multimillion-dollar technology projects in the Fortune 100 market space—giving him a robust set of experiences.

In addition to his bachelor's degree in sociology and his master's degree in social policy planning, Paul has also spent over 20 years studying martial arts, bushido, qigong, Eastern philosophy, practical psychology, linguistics, and human awareness. He brings a rich and profound understanding of what makes people tick and leverages this understanding to heighten the business/organizational experience and increase revenue and profits.

What makes Paul's work different is his approach: He creates the space to hold people's human concerns while they fulfill their business requirements. This is authenticity in action, producing both immediate and long-term benefits. Paul's approach never forgets that business is always about two very important things: revenue and people. He never thinks of one without the other.

The Wha-Dho Sales Strategy

In 2003 Paul decided to standardize and systematize the principles of the **Wha-Dho** philosophy to developing a sales strategy that would work in all markets, particularly a changing one. He created a **Wha-Dho** sales strategy that leveraged these three elements:

1. The Human Capital within your organization.
2. Economic Principles that apply to your business.
3. Business Practices that relate to your industry.

Paul used the resulting dynamic as a sales strategy to help companies increase revenue and profit margins. Here are some of his success stories:

- A manufacturer of spectrophotometers in Athens, Georgia—Increased revenue 60% in 18 months.
- A contract manufacturer in Santa Clara, California—Increased revenue 300% in 24 months.
- A 40-year-old printing company in San Mateo, California—Increased revenue 20% in 12 months.

Despite the industry verticals, the rules of business remain the same. At a fundamental level, Paul's success is a result of what is possible when these three elements—human capital, economic principles, and business practices—come together:

Invitation to Participate

Paul invites you to visit his Web site, www.pauldsouza.com, and participate in the online community he is developing as a resource to help sales professionals enhance their careers. Visit and share your experiences!

Introducing the USEF

I would like to take the opportunity to introduce you to the University Sales Education Foundation (USEF). They are doing fantastic work in nurturing the professionalism of sales in the United States and throughout the world. The overall mission of the USEF is to promote the profession of sales and its role as the driving force in the economy. Our goal is to increase the number of schools that offer USEF-approved professional sales education by 10% each year. Please consider working with them and the many affiliate universities that offer sales programs when you seek to augment your sales organization.

I have talked to a number of sales leaders and hiring managers, including Jeremy Tudor, a Program Director at AT&T, who is in charge of recruiting and training new sales hires nationwide. He says that AT&T saves tens of thousands of dollars per employee in training and other related costs, as well as achieving a shorter ramp to productivity and better recruiting results, when hiring graduates of USEF programs. Take advantage of these benefits and help us develop the profession of sales, the heartbeat of all business.

Find the USEF on the Web at www.saleseducationfoundation.org.

Acknowledgements

This book is a manifestation of our commitment to serve. We seek to help people live powerful lives, ones conducted with harmony and prosperity. I have to start this process by giving my friend Rajesh Setty a big thank you for helping me commit myself to writing a book; your coaching, guidance, and prodding me along are much appreciated. Not often do we come across people who help change our lives, and I appreciate all that you have done for me. Your persistence over the last five years has paid off. It has been a fantastic experience and I have thoroughly enjoyed it.

I am extremely grateful to my support team that has helped me put this book together. Bill Sherman, I could not have done this without you. Your patience and guidance helped me shape the message. James Wondrack, your sense of design brought light and life to the project. Ceil Goldman, thank you for crossing my t's and dotting my i's. I know that you know I needed you. David Wilk, my publisher, you have helped me make sense of this business and helped create the infrastructure needed to make this book a reality.

For all my friends who helped me in the early stages of writing this book, I cannot thank you enough. You helped me shape my message and improve the quality of my story; you saw the diamond in the rough in all the very rough drafts I sent you. Tom Beans, Gil Boncy, Hanley Brite, Linda Bunner, Denis Clark, Gerard Das, Terry Grundy, Ben Harris, Doug May, August Nazareth, Dan Perry, Peter Purshotma, Parker Thomson, Arun Nithyanandam, and Jared Wills.

I loved you all for being there for me and giving me your honest feedback. A big thank you to my mother Christine D'Souza; she read every word and gave me her feedback along the way—even helping to evangelize presales of the book in Elberton, Georgia.

Writing a book is no small feat. I have been humbled by the process, yet there have been people in the recent past who have helped me realize that I have an important message that needs to be told. My heartfelt thank you for that feedback and support to Chip Conley, Leyton Cougar, Chris Derry, Don Elliott, Mark Foust, Karla Maans Giroux, Gerhard Gschwandtner, Lisa Haneberg, Irina Haydon and Richard Cisneros, Mahaveer Jain, Scott Marker, Bill Palmer, David Parks, Mark Sellers, Steve Shapiro, Howard Stevens, and Jim Switzenberg. You all have been extremely supportive in your willingness to share your thoughts, ideas, and support with me.

A special thanks to Ashok in Chennai, India; I appreciate your friendship and guidance through these years. You helped me write the appropriate first book.

A big thank you to Kegan, Kelly, Christle and others at the FedEx Kinko's office in Montgomery, Ohio; for taking care of me with my many last minute "special" requests.

None of this would have been possible without my wife and family. My wife, Shino, has been an angel, tolerating my long hours away from things we usually do together. Shino, I appreciate your constant care and the sharing of our vision for life.

And, of course, my thanks for all the support from the rest of the family—in Japan, Australia, Georgia, and India. I love you guys and could not have done this without you.

166

Use this space to take notes and design a powerful future as you read this book.

_____

_____

_____

_____

_____

_____

_____

_____

_____

_____

_____

_____

_____

Reality is a state of mind,
people don't see life as it is,
they see life as they are.